SIX MONTHS

New Zealand and the Covid-19 Pandemic

January - June 2020

A Timeline of Events

Written and Compiled

by

Jason Komene

For

Liz and Logan,

And...

The team of Five Million.

FOREWORD

June 8, 2020. 100 days after New Zealand reported its first case of Covid-19, and 75 days after imposing the Alert Level 4 Lockdown, the New Zealand Government declared that there were no more active cases of Covid-19 in the country. Effectively we'd eliminated community transmission of the virus; the first country in the world to have significant case numbers and do so.

Forewarned by what we were seeing around the world, a team of 5 million New Zealanders were called upon by the New Zealand Government to take on an invisible enemy threatening to kill vulnerable members of our community. 'Go Early and Go Hard,' was our response to the virus and no one was exempt from the cause. The team of 5 million included every New Zealander, young and old, all with a common goal: Eliminate Covid-19.

There would be 1504 cases before elimination... And 22 people would die.

Scientifically based, the New Zealand response was formulated by medical experts who kept the health of the population in mind. Through almost daily briefings, Jacinda Ardern, (the New Zealand Prime Minister), and Ashley Bloomfield, (the New Zealand Director-General of Health), delivered the latest developments of the Covid-19 response in a simple clear language that all the country could understand.

Border closures saw our tourism industry collapse. Lockdown saw many businesses go under and a lot of people lose their jobs. There were many sacrifices but we understood that we were doing what needed to be done to rid our country of the disease. We gave up the freedom to visit family and friends, play sport, travel freely, and attend weddings or funerals. Everyday we tuned in to hear the latest case numbers. The daily results convinced us that we were on the right track and we could beat this thing.

And in the end we did.

It took a hundred days.

What follows is a six-month day-by-day account of the Covid-19 virus and what it was doing to the world; how it snuck up on us while our attention was focussed on Australian fires. It shows the speed in which the virus swept across the globe, bringing death to almost everywhere it touched. It portrays Covid-19 as a wildfire more reaching and devastating than the Australian bushfires, with countries and territories falling like dominoes before it. And it presents the number of cases accelerating beyond belief. Because I'm a Kiwi New Zealand gets particular attention.

Not everything is here. That would be impossible. Every country had its own story to tell and I couldn't cover everything. I'm not omnipotent, but the Internet pretty much is. There's an endless amount of information on there. Everyone seems to have an opinion and some of those opinions range from the sensible to the stupid to the downright dangerous. Sometimes the lines got blurred and it was hard to know what to believe. I've kept away from the numerous Conspiracy Theories surrounding the Covid-19 pandemic, only drawing on them if they became pertinent to the events of the day.

Covid-19 is ongoing, as is the information surrounding it. Not all has yet been revealed, (and a lot may never be). Investigations and discoveries continue to reveal things that happened weeks or months ago, so the past is still being written. As for the future...? Covid-19 has shown us that we can't predict what is just around the corner. We have no idea what it will throw at us tomorrow, let alone next week.

This is the first six months.

Jason Komene   14 July, 2020.

JANUARY 2020

JANUARY 1
WEDNESDAY

(AUS) Thousands of people have lost their homes in Australia as the worst bush fires in years continue to rage throughout the country. There are large parts of Victoria and New South Wales that have been devastated. About 4000 people are trapped on a beach on the South Coast of Australia. Smoke from the fires are reaching New Zealand 2000km away.

(CH) China has notified the World Health Organisation of several cases of an unusual pneumonia appearing in a Port City called Wuhan. Several of the infections are linked to the Huanan Seafood Wholesale Market in Wuhan City. The Market has been closed down.

JANUARY 2
THURSDAY

(AUS) The Royal Australian Navy has rescued thousands of people trapped on beaches by the bushfires.

(CH) 41 patients have been admitted to hospitals in Wuhan with pneumonia. 66% of them had direct contact with the Huanan Seafood Wholesale Market.

(IRAN) Iran's top security and intelligence commander, Qasem Suleimani, has been killed in a drone strike authorised by President Trump. United States officials are braced for potential Iranian retaliatory attacks.

(NZ) Glaciers and Mountains in the South Island of New Zealand are turning brown from smoke, ash, and dust drifting over the Tasman Sea from the bushfires in Australia.

JANUARY 3 FRIDAY

(AUS) It's been estimated that half a billion animals (500 million!!) have perished in the Australian bushfires since they began.

(CH) China officially informs the World Health Organisation, and relevant countries and regions, (Hong Kong, Macao, and Taiwan), about the pneumonia outbreak in Wuhan.

(CH) On December 30th, last year, a Chinese doctor named Li Wenliang sent a message to his medical school contacts informing them of an unknown virus seen in seven patients. All of the patients had either worked or visited the Wuhan Seafood Wholesale Market. Today he was summoned to a Police Station where Authorities told him that his warning was illegal, and it had 'severely disturbed the social order.' He was told to sign a letter that said: 'We solemnly warn you: If you keep being stubborn, with such impertinence, and continue this illegal activity, you will be brought to justice – is that understood?' He signed and was then allowed to return to work.

JANUARY 4
SATURDAY

(AUS) The fires are still blazing in Australia. There are reports that the whole of Kangaroo Island is now under threat. Two people on Kangaroo Island have died, bringing the total number of bushfire deaths this summer to 21.

JANUARY 5 SUNDAY

(AUS) A lot of people are attributing the fires in Australia to Climate Change, but not Scott Morrison, the Australian Prime Minister. Last year he said that there was no credible link between climate change and the bushfires. A few days ago he visited victims in Cobargo, New South Wales; he was not warmly welcomed by the locals. Scott Morrison has been heavily criticised for taking his family on an overseas holiday to Hawaii last month, while the bushfires were still raging.

(AUS/US) Pop star Pink has tweeted that she is donating $500,000 to Australian Firefighters.

(CH) SARS, Bird Flu and Middle East Respiratory Syndrome have all been ruled out as the mysterious viral pneumonia continues to infect people in central China.

JANUARY 6 MONDAY

(IRAN) Hundreds of thousands of people have taken to the streets of Tehran for the funeral of Qasem Soleimani, who was killed in a drone attack last Thursday.

JANUARY 7 TUESDAY

(CH) In China a new type of Coronavirus has been identified and isolated by the Authorities. (It has been called "Novel Coronavirus" or nCoV).

(IRAN) A deadly stampede crush at the burial of Qasem Soleimani in Kerman, has killed 50 people and injured more than 200 others.

JANUARY 8
WEDNESDAY

(AUS) In New South Wales Australian Police have rounded up 24 alleged arsonists accused of deliberately starting bushfires.

(NZ) People travelling on the Interislander Ferry that sails between the North and South Islands may have been exposed to Measles over the holiday period. Those that travelled on certain dates have been asked to self-isolate; some until January 20. Last year New Zealand recorded over 2000 cases of measles – more than what was recorded in the entire United States. The New Zealand Measles Outbreak spread to other countries, most notably Samoa where more than 70 people died.

JANUARY 9
THURSDAY

(CH) A 61 year-old man has died of respiratory failure caused by severe pneumonia, in the city of Wuhan, China.

(NZ) Hawkes Bay Firefighters have been fighting a blaze for three days.

JANUARY 10 FRIDAY

(UK) A lot of Royal watchers in the United Kingdom and around the world are shocked that Prince Harry and Meghan Markle have announced that they plan to 'step back' from Royal duties.

JANUARY 11
SATURDAY

(WHO) The World Health Organisation received information today from the National Health Commission in China that the outbreak is associated with one seafood market in Wuhan City.

(UK) The Queen of England is said to be more angry with Harry and Meghan 'stepping back' from Royal duties than Prince Andrew's disastrous interview last November concerning the Epstein scandal. Jeffrey Epstein was a convicted sex offender who had a lot of important friends, including the Prince. Last year in July he was arrested on charges of sex trafficking of minors in Florida and New York. He committed suicide in his jail cell in August. There's a damning photo of Prince Andrew with his arm around a 17 year-old girl taken in 2001 at the home of Epstein's former girlfriend, Ghislaine Maxwell. The 17 year-old, (now 35), has alleged that she was procured by Ghislaine Maxwell as a teenage sex slave for Jeffrey Epstein and that she had sex with Prince Andrew. Jeffrey Epstein supposedly took the photo. Prince Andrew's interview last year was described as a train wreck where he denied having sex with the 17 year-old, adding that he had no regret over his friendship with Epstein.

JANUARY 12 SUNDAY

(AUS) Serena Williams has won the ASB Classic in Auckland. She is donating all of her prize money (US$43,000) to Australian bushfire relief efforts.

(CH) China has shared the genetic sequence of the Novel Coronavirus for other countries to use in developing diagnostic kits.

JANUARY 13 MONDAY

(GLOBAL) The Coronavirus has gone International with cases reported outside of China...

(THAILAND) A 61-year-old woman is in hospital with a case of pneumonia similar to that seen in China.

(USA) The United States have their first case of the Coronavirus.

(NZ) Because of the bushfires in Australia a petition has been signed by over 4000 people to allow koalas to be introduced into New Zealand.

JANUARY 14
TUESDAY

(NZ) A report from an Australian academic says that New Zealand should be reminded of the introduction of possums before considering introducing koalas. With the introduction of koalas there's a possibility that not only could they displace some of our native species but they could also bring in some new exotic disease.

JANUARY 15
WEDNESDAY

(CH) In China infrared thermometers have been installed in airports, railway stations, long-distance bus stations and ferry terminals.

(CH) A second person has died in Wuhan from the new virus. He was 69 years old.

(NZ) A group of Scientists in Auckland have made a world-first breakthrough that could help treat dementia. A study has found that tiny star-shaped cells called Astrocytes control blood flow to the brain. Disturbances to blood flow in the brain are the main proponents of diseases like dementia and Alzheimer's. Studies are ongoing but they hope to move on to clinical trials in the next few years.

JANUARY 16
THURSDAY

(JAPAN) Japan records its first case of the coronavirus.

(THAILAND) Thailand reports its second case of the coronavirus.

(NZ) 116 Defence Force staff have been deployed to Australia to help deal with the fires. Some have been assigned to removing the carcasses of wildlife from Kangaroo Island.

JANUARY 17 FRIDAY

(AUS) While fires continue to rage across Australia torrential rain has hit parts of Queensland and New South Wales. Flash flooding has caused power outages and road closures.

JANUARY 18
SATURDAY

(CH) A third man in Wuhan has died.
(UK) Prince Harry and Meghan have lost their HRH titles. This means that they will no longer be receiving public funds.

JANUARY 19 SUNDAY

(NZ) There are no plans to introduce thermal screening at airports in New Zealand. The Ministry of Health has said that research has shown thermal screening to be generally ineffective in the detection of influenza.

JANUARY 20 MONDAY

(ASIA) 282 confirmed cases of the Coronavirus have been reported from four different Asian countries. China has 278 of the cases, (258 from Hubei Province), Thailand has 2 cases, and Japan and South Korea each have 1 case.

(S KOREA) South Korea has its first case of the Coronavirus.

JANUARY 21
TUESDAY

(NZ) News of a new coronavirus continues to be mentioned in news reports. The new coronavirus originates in China where it's just been confirmed that the virus can be transmitted from human to human. There are almost 300 people infected in China, and cases have been discovered in other countries.

(TAIWAN) Taiwan has its first case of the Coronavirus.

JANUARY 22
WEDNESDAY

(CH) China has quarantined Wuhan City where the coronavirus originated.

(N KOREA) To protect against the new virus North Korea has closed its borders to all foreign tourists.

(CANADA) Canada has its first case of the Coronavirus.

(MACAU) Macau has its first case of the Coronavirus.

JANUARY 23
THURSDAY

(CH) The virus has claimed the lives of 17 people in China. There are now more than 500 people infected, although there are fears that the actual number could be closer to 10,000 as China might be under-reporting infections. It's possible that the new virus could be as deadly as the 'Spanish Flu' epidemic that killed up to 50 million people early last century.

(HONG KONG) Hong Kong has its first case of the Coronavirus.

(NEPAL) Nepal has its first case of the Coronavirus.

(SINGAPORE) Singapore has its first case of the Coronavirus.

(VIETNAM) Vietnam has its first case of the Coronavirus.

JANUARY 24 FRIDAY

(CH) Foxes and koalas were just two of the exotic animals sold at the food market in Wuhan, the epicentre of the Coronavirus Outbreak. All of the animals on sale were for human consumption!

(FRANCE) The first Coronavirus case in Europe is recorded in Bordeaux, France. Two further cases are later confirmed in Paris.

(NZ) Health Minister David Clark says that the Ministry of Health have been actively monitoring the Coronavirus situation since the 6th of January. New Zealand's response at this stage is: 'alert but not alarmed.' The Ministry has triggered a pandemic response in line with their pandemic plan; a plan that is regularly updated.

(SWEDEN) Sweden has its first case of the Coronavirus.

JANUARY 25
SATURDAY

(C-19) Coronaviruses are named for the spikes that protrude from their membranes. There are many different Coronaviruses that can infect animals or people, (sometimes both). Coronaviruses cause illnesses of the respiratory tract, ranging from the common cold to severe conditions like SARS. The coronavirus that originated in Wuhan has symptoms of infection that include: a high fever; difficulty breathing; and lung lesions. Milder cases may resemble the flu or a bad cold. The incubation period is believed to be about two weeks.

(AUS) Australia has reported its first case of Coronavirus in Melbourne, Victoria.

(CH) A doctor in Hubei Province has died from the virus. He was 62 years old and was at the front line of the outbreak in Wuhan City.

(CH) China has begun building a 1000-bed emergency hospital. It will solely be used for people infected with the coronavirus. They expect the build to take ten days and be completed by February 3rd.

(MALAYSIA) Malaysia has recorded its first three cases of Coronavirus.

(NZ) Over 100 students from Wuhan are expected to arrive in NZ for University studies. There are currently no restrictions on travel. The Ministry of Health says the risk in New Zealand is low.

JANUARY 26 SUNDAY

(GLOBAL) There are fifteen countries and territories now with confirmed cases of Coronavirus. (China, Thailand, The United States, Japan, South Korea, Taiwan, Macau, Canada, Vietnam, Hong Kong, Singapore, Sweden, France, Australia and Malaysia). At least 41 people have died, (all in China). Globally more than 1200 people are infected.

(AUS) Four coronavirus cases have been confirmed in Australia. All of the cases are related to people who have just flown in from China.

(CH) China has banned the trade of wild animals, (in markets and online), throughout the country.

(HONG KONG) Hong Kong has stated that from tomorrow it will ban anyone who has been to Hubei Province in the last 14 days.

(NZ) A public health nurse will be based at both the Auckland and Christchurch airports to take the temperature of incoming passengers from China who feel ill.

JANUARY 27 MONDAY

(C-19) Studies have shown that the majority of people who have died from the virus have been in their late 50's or older.

(MONGOLIA) Mongolia has closed its border with China and shut down all schools until March 2nd.

(NZ) Rumours of a possible Coronavirus case in Queenstown have proven false. The Queenstown Mayor is urging New Zealanders to continue welcoming overseas tourists and not to descend to racism or xenophobia.

(US) Kobe Bryant of LA Lakers fame has been killed in a helicopter crash. One of his daughters was with him and was also killed.

(CAMBODIA) Cambodia has its first case of the Coronavirus.

(GERMANY) Germany has its first case of the Coronavirus

(SRI LANKA) Sri Lanka has its first case of the Coronavirus.

JANUARY 28
TUESDAY

(GLOBAL) Markets around the world have been hit by the spread of the deadly Coronavirus. Japan's Nikkei index shed 2%; it's biggest one-day drop in 5 months. In Europe 586 stocks on the pan-European 600 Stoxx index are in the red. Wall Street futures are pointing to falls of 1.4% on the S and P 500 and the Dow Jones. The UK's FTSE is down 185 points.

(FIJI) Six people are being quarantined in Fiji after being refused entry into Samoa. Samoa was ravaged by a measles epidemic last year and is taking no chances with these six. Each failed to meet Samoa's quarantine requirements by not having the appropriate medical clearances. Samoa's restrictions require anyone who's been in China to 'self quarantine' for 14 days in a country that is free of the Coronavirus. Fiji examined the six and they all tested OK with no fever.

(NZ) The Director-General of Health, Dr Ashley Bloomfield, has said that there is a high likelihood of New Zealand getting a case of the virus. Based on current information the likelihood of a sustained community outbreak is low.

(NZ) In Auckland some schools are telling students who have returned from countries with confirmed coronavirus cases to miss the start of term and stay home for 2 weeks.

(UK) The Foreign Office has issued a warning for Britons not to travel to Mainland China unless the journey is essential.

JANUARY 29
WEDNESDAY

(GLOBAL) According to a Global Health Security Index survey of pandemic preparedness, (released last October), out of 195 countries New Zealand comes in 35th, (tied with Hungary). There are 34 countries in the world better prepared to handle a possible pandemic than New Zealand. In order they are: 1 – USA. 2 – UK. 3 – Netherlands. 4 – Australia. 5 – Canada. 6 – Thailand. 7 – Sweden. 8 – Denmark. 9 – South Korea. 10 – Finland. 11 – France. 12 – Slovenia. 13 – Switzerland. 14 – Germany. 15 – Spain. 16 – Norway. 17 – Latvia. 18 – Malaysia. 19 – Belgium. 20 – Portugal. 21 – Japan. 22 – Brazil. 23 – Ireland. 24 – Singapore. 25 – Argentina. 26 – Austria. 27 – Chile. 28 – Mexico. 29 – Estonia. 30 – Indonesia. 31 – Italy. 32 – Poland. 33 – Lithuania. 34 – South Africa.

(C-19) A "novel Coronavirus" refers to a NEW Coronavirus that has not been previously identified.

(CANADA) The Canadian Government has issued a travel advisory to avoid non-essential travel to China; and avoid all travel to the province of Hubei.

(NZ) 163 New Zealanders are registered as being in Wuhan, the epicentre of the Coronavirus outbreak in China.

(PAPUA NEW GUINEA) Papua New Guinea has closed its border with Indonesia and banned all travellers from Asian countries.

(US) 195 Americans have been evacuated from Wuhan. They have been instructed to remain for three days in an Air Force base in Southern California, where they will all be evaluated. Once cleared they will be allowed to fly home, where for 14 days they will be monitored by local medical teams.

(FINLAND) Finland has its first case of the Coronavirus.

(UNITED ARAB EMIRATES) The United Arab Emirates have their first case of the Coronavirus.

JANUARY 30
THURSDAY

(WHO) The World Health Organisation has declared the Coronavirus outbreak a Public Health Emergency of International Concern. There are now more than 9000 cases in China and 98 cases in other countries. 170 people have died, all of them in China.

(NZ) The Government will charter an Air New Zealand plane to assist New Zealanders wanting to leave Wuhan. Health Officials are currently working out where to quarantine them.

(UK) British Airways has stopped flying to or from China. They join other international airlines, (United Airlines, Air Asia, Cathay Pacific, Air India, Lufthansa, and Finnair), who have either stopped or reduced flights to China.

(INDIA) India has its first case of the Coronavirus.

(PHILIPPINES) The Philippines have their first case of Coronavirus.

JANUARY 31 FRIDAY

(WHO) The Director-General of the World Health Organisation, Tedros Adhanom, has said that there is no reason for measures that unnecessarily interfere with International Travel and Trade.

(RUSSIA) Russian authorities have extended their border closure with China until at least March 1st.

(SINGAPORE) Singapore has closed its borders to all visitors from Mainland China, including people transiting through Singapore. Residents and long-term visa holders will be allowed to return.

(US) President Trump has banned foreign nationals from entering the United States if they have been in China within the last two weeks.

(ITALY) Italy has its first two cases of Coronavirus.

(RUSSIA) Russia has its first case of the Coronavirus.

(SPAIN) Spain has its first case of the Coronavirus.

(UK) The United Kingdom has its first case of the Coronavirus.

(GLOBAL) The following 27 countries and territories have reported cases of the Coronavirus: Australia; Cambodia; Canada; China; Finland; France; Germany; Hong Kong; India; Italy; Japan; Macau; Malaysia; Nepal; Philippines; Russia; Singapore; Spain; Sweden; South Korea; Sri Lanka; Taiwan; Thailand; the United Arab Emirates; the United Kingdom; the United States of America; and Vietnam.

(GLOBAL) There may be other countries with cases but they may not have started testing for the virus yet.

JANUARY:
YESTERDAY'S NEWS

I won't lie to you.

This will sound callous, (now that we all know better), but in January I wasn't too bothered with the virus-thing happening in China. I don't think many of us in New Zealand were, if we're being honest. China was over 10,000km away and the virus-thing was surely 'somebody else's problem.' Before it got anywhere near New Zealand it would be either contained or fizzle away like last year's flu. It had happened before and there was no reason to think that it wouldn't happen again and become yesterday's news.

The first time I heard anything about the virus it was January the 21st. I was camping with friends and family, where, as a rule we tried to stay away from everything, and that, included the news. But the news found us. By the time we heard about the mystery-virus people were dying; but hey, people die everyday. Our news broadcasts gravitate to the fact of this. On a daily basis we're kept informed of the latest natural disasters, car crashes, shootings, explosions, etc. and the associated number of people who have died. The number of deaths associated with this new virus was low, (on January 21st it was about 10, Worldwide!). Although any death of course is a tragedy, that number hardly seemed worthy of the amount of attention the media was placing on this new virus. After all, ten people aren't a lot when you consider that in New Zealand ten people die every two days of heart attacks.

As far as a new virus was concerned, well, the bad ones don't tend to jump too many borders before they're stopped in their tracks. After all, Zika and Ebola never reached us. Swine flu and Bird flu sort of got close but were we truly ever in any danger here in New Zealand? Those two fizzled away and life went on. Our economists were worried but the rest of us probably didn't take too much notice.

In January all of our concern was on our Australian neighbours across the Tasman Sea. Australia was on fire, and had been for months. The deadly fires had destroyed homes and killed millions of animals. Footage of smouldering koalas and kangaroos fleeing before blankets of flame was far more visual, and visceral, than anything we were seeing coming out of China, which appeared cleansed and sanitised by comparison. The new Coronavirus couldn't compete. The Australian fires had all of us riveted. And although Australia was a few thousand kilometres away we were still catching their smoke.

So I won't lie to you.

China was a country far far away. And their little virus-thing... well, surely it would just fizzle away.

Jason Komene 5 April, 2020

FEBRUARY 2020

FEBRUARY 1
SATURDAY

(GLOBAL) More than 11,000 people around the world have been infected. 259 of these have died, all of them in China.

(NZ) New Zealand has its first 'suspected' case of Coronavirus. The person has been tested and the results are due tomorrow.

(NZ) Air New Zealand has announced that it will stop its flights between Shanghai and Auckland from February 9.

(NZ) According to New Zealand's online auction site, TradeMe, there have been 22,000 searches for the term: 'Facemask.'

(US) American Airlines are pulling out of China following pressure from their pilots.

FEBRUARY 2 SUNDAY

(CH) Construction of the new 1000-bed Hospital in Wuhan has been completed within ten days.

(NZ) Test results for New Zealand's first possible Coronavirus case have come back negative.

(NZ) Analysts are forecasting that the New Zealand economy will take a significant hit that's likely to be in the hundreds of millions. They forecast a loss of $300 million by the end of March.

(NZ) 10,000 Chinese visitors have cancelled their trips to New Zealand. Tourism New Zealand says this is likely only the tip of the iceberg.

(PHILIPPINES) The first death outside of China has been recorded in the Philippines.

FEBRUARY 3 MONDAY

(CH) Chinese Stock Markets have plunged on the first trading day after the Lunar New Year.

(NZ) The New Zealand Government has placed entry restrictions on all foreign nationals travelling from, or transiting through, Mainland China. These restrictions will remain in place for up to 14 days, reviewed every 48 hours. New Zealand citizens and permanent residents returning from China will be allowed to enter but will be required to self-isolate for 14 days on arrival.

(US) The first person in the United States infected with the virus has recovered and left hospital.

(BELGIUM) Belgium has its first case of the Coronavirus.

FEBRUARY 4 TUESDAY

(HONG KONG) Hong Kong has reported the second Coronavirus death outside of Mainland China.

(NZ) Air New Zealand flight 6001 is flying to Wuhan in China to evacuate New Zealanders that are trapped there. The plane has the capacity to hold up to 300 people so some other travellers stuck in Wuhan will be offered a flight out as well. Anyone who is feeling unwell will not be permitted to board the flight.

(TAIWAN) Taiwan has banned all foreign nationals who have been to China in the last 14 days.

FEBRUARY 5
WEDNESDAY

(NZ) The 193 people evacuated on the Air New Zealand flight from Wuhan have arrived safely in Auckland. 23 Australian citizens and 12 Australian permanent residents took the flight as well. They will be flown to Australia while all the other passengers are quarantined for 14 days in Whangaparaoa. One person was turned away from the flight because they were ill.

(US) The CDC (Centers for Disease Control and Prevention) has begun shipping out test kits to more than 100 labs across the United States.

FEBRUARY 6
THURSDAY

(ITALY) Italy has its third Coronavirus case.

(JAPAN) It has been confirmed that twenty people on board a cruise-ship called the Diamond Princess have tested positive for Coronavirus. The ship is off the coast of Japan and is carrying 2666 passengers and 1045 crew. 13 of the passengers are from New Zealand.

FEBRUARY 7 FRIDAY

(GLOBAL) There are now more than 28,000 confirmed cases in the world. That's 20,000 more than a week ago! 14 of those cases are in Australia. The official worldwide death toll is 565.

(GLOBAL) The Chief Executive of the Tokyo Olympics is extremely concerned about how the virus could affect the Summer Games this year. The Tokyo Olympics are scheduled to begin on the 24th of July and run through to the 9th of August.

(C-19) Although the Coronavirus death toll is steadily increasing it's been noted that the death rate, (about 2 per cent), is well below the mortality rate of SARS, responsible for killing about 800 people in 2002 – 2003.

(CH) Li Wenliang, the doctor who tried to issue the first warning about the Coronavirus, has died of the disease. On 10th January he'd developed a cough, the next day he had a fever and two days later he was in hospital.

(US) The United States has announced that it's prepared to spend $100 million to assist China and other impacted countries.

FEBRUARY 8
SATURDAY

(CH) Another makeshift hospital has been opened in Wuhan, providing an extra 1500 beds for virus patients. The authorities have been converting buildings into hospitals to deal with the high number of infections.

(CH) The Chinese media announce that the virus can be spread via aerosol transmission. This means that the virus can drift through the air for an extended period of time, causing infection if breathed in. Later...

(CH) The Chinese reverse their earlier claim that the virus can be spread by aerosol transmission, saying that there is no definitive answer to whether the virus is airborne.

(C-19) Currently Coronavirus has only two known modes of transmission. Direct and Contact.

- Direct Transmission occurs when a person breathes the air close to an infected person who has sneezed or coughed.
- Contact Transmission is when a person touches a contaminated surface and then they touch their mouth, eyes or nose.

(JAPAN) Off the coast of Japan 64 people on the Diamond Princess Cruise-ship have tested positive.

FEBRUARY 9 SUNDAY

(CH) The death toll in China has surpassed the number of people who died from SARS in the SARS epidemic of 2002-2003. SARS killed 774 people. This new virus has killed 908.

(JAPAN) Passengers on the Diamond Princess Cruise-ship are confined to their cabins but are allowed on deck for an hour.

FEBRUARY 10
MONDAY

(WHO) A team of World Health Organisation medical experts have arrived in China.

(JAPAN) There are 135 cases of Covid-19 on the Diamond Princess Cruise-ship.

(NZ) Pharmacies are selling out of facemasks and hand sanitizer. Soon there will be a shortage in New Zealand. Because of demand the prices of facemasks on TradeMe have shot up to ridiculous prices; in some cases $50/mask.

FEBRUARY 11
TUESDAY

(GLOBAL) The death toll for the Coronavirus has passed 1000. There are now 1115 deaths due to the Coronavirus.

(GLOBAL) Catching the Coronavirus is not necessarily a death sentence. 4803 people have recovered from the virus.

(WHO) The World Health Organisation has announced that the Official name of the Coronavirus will be COVID-19. Short for COrona VIrus Disease 2019. While the disease is called Covid-19 the virus that causes it is named: Severe Acute Respiratory Syndrome Coronavirus 2 or SARS-CoV-2. The virus was initially referred to as the 2019 Novel Coronavirus or 2019-n-CoV.

(US) The first group of Americans evacuated from Wuhan have been released from Quarantine.

FEBRUARY 12
WEDNESDAY

(C-19) Scientists are confused as to why out of 965 cases in China less than 2% of them occurred in children under 19 years of age.

They suggest two possibilities:

1. Covid-19 is less likely to infect children, or
2. Children exhibit milder symptoms or none at all.

(JAPAN) There are now 175 cases of Covid-19 on the Diamond Princess Cruise-ship.

FEBRUARY 13
THURSDAY

(JAPAN) 218 people have tested positive for Covid-19 on the Diamond Princess Cruise-ship.

FEBRUARY 14 FRIDAY

(CH) More than 1700 health workers in China have been infected by Covid-19.

(CH) Beijing has announced that everyone returning to the city will have to self-quarantine for 14 days. Those that do not will be punished.

(JAPAN) Virus-free passengers have been allowed to disembark the Diamond Princess Cruise-ship to complete their isolation in Japanese Government housing.

(EGYPT) Egypt has its first case of the Coronavirus.

FEBRUARY 15
SATURDAY

(CH) 760 million people in China are in Lockdowns.

(FRANCE) France has reported the 4th death from Covid-19 outside of Mainland China. It's the first death in Europe.

(US) The United States is planning to evacuate about 400 virus-free Americans quarantined on the Diamond Princess Cruise-ship.

FEBRUARY 16
SUNDAY

(AUS) Alice Cooper, Queen/Adam Lambert, and Ronan Keating, have joined other musical acts in a huge concert called Fire Fight Australia. It has been organised to raise money for those affected by the Australian fires. Other artists on the bill include: John Farnham, Guy Sebastian, Delta Goodrem, Icehouse, 5 Seconds Of Summer, and k.d. Laing.

(JAPAN) Japan confirms that there are 373 cases of Covid-19 aboard the Diamond Princess Cruise-ship.

(NZ) Fears over the Coronavirus outbreak have driven customers away from many Chinese restaurants.

FEBRUARY 17
MONDAY

(C-19) Out of 45,000 confirmed cases in China only one person under the age of 20 has died. There have been no deaths among children younger than 10. Because children are not developing major symptoms the number of cases in children is likely to be under-reported. Dr Arthur Reingold, a Californian epidemiologist, says that we have to assume that children are spreading it. He says that school closures will at least delay the peak of the outbreak.

(JAPAN) Japan confirms another 99 cases of Covid-19 on board the Diamond Princess Cruise-ship. The number of cases is now 443.

(NZ) Elton John has cancelled the rest of his New Zealand concerts after being diagnosed with 'walking pneumonia.' Last night he couldn't finish an Auckland concert. It's been a busy few weeks for Sir Elton. He played concerts in New Zealand, then instantly flew to the United States to perform at the Academy Awards, then returned to complete his New Zealand tour.

FEBRUARY 18
TUESDAY

(C-19) What's known about Covid-19 so far:
1. It has Flu-like symptoms including fever and coughing.
2. In some patients (particularly the elderly and others with chronic health conditions) the above symptoms can develop into pneumonia with chest tightness, chest pain and shortness of breath.
3. It seems to start with a Fever, followed by a dry cough. After a week it can lead to shortness of breath with about 20% of patients requiring hospital treatment.
4. It rarely seems to cause a runny nose, sneezing or a sore throat.
5. 80% of cases are mild and can recover at home.
6. 13.8% of cases are severe, developing pneumonia and shortness of breath.
7. 4.7% of cases are critical and can include: respiratory failure, septic shock and multi-organ failure.
8. The risk of death increases with age.
9. Relatively few cases have been seen among children.
10. As it's a 'Novel Coronavirus,' no one is immune.

(JAPAN) Japan confirms 88 more cases on the Diamond Princess Cruise-ship, raising the total to 542.

(RUSSIA) Russia has banned all Chinese citizens from entering the country.

FEBRUARY 19
WEDNESDAY

(GLOBAL) The global death toll has surpassed 2000 cases. 2126 people have now died from the virus.

(GLOBAL) 16,357 people have recovered from Covid-19.

(C-19) The most effective ways to protect yourself, (and others), from Covid-19 are:

1. Cover your cough or sneeze using a tissue or your elbow. NOT your hand.
2. Wash your hands with soap for twenty seconds. Then dry them.
3. Stay at least 2 meters away from other people.
4. Regularly clean surfaces that might have been touched.
5. Regularly clean surfaces you have touched.
6. Avoid shaking hands, or touching your face without first washing your hands.

(JAPAN) Japan confirms another 79 Covid-19 cases on the Diamond Princess Cruise-ship. The total number of cases so far is 621.

(JAPAN) A Japanese health expert has been on the Diamond Princess Cruise-ship and described the situation on board as completely chaotic. Passengers who are virus-free have been allowed to disembark since the 14th of February, to continue their isolation on shore.

(IRAN) Iran has its first case of the Coronavirus.

FEBRUARY 20
THURSDAY

(JAPAN) Two of the passengers that were on board the Diamond Princess Cruise-ship have died. 13 more cases have been confirmed today, bringing the total to 634.

(KUWAIT) Kuwait has suspended all flights of Kuwait Airlines to Iran. Iran reported its first case yesterday.

FEBRUARY 21 FRIDAY

(ITALY) Italy has reported its first death from Covid-19. It comes as 16 cases are reported in Lombardy. Italy has been sitting on 3 cases for the last two weeks.

(JAPAN) Large gatherings will be suspended in Japan until at least mid-March.

(ISRAEL) Israel has its first case of the Coronavirus.

(LEBANON) Lebanon has its first case of the Coronavirus.

FEBRUARY 22
SATURDAY

(WHO) The World Health Organisation joint mission of experts, (that have been in China since February 10), have arrived in Wuhan.

(ITALY) There are 60 more cases in Italy bringing their case numbers to 79 infections. 54 of these have been found in Lombardy, 17 in Veneto, 2 in Emilia Romagno, 2 in Lazio, and 1 in Piedmont.

(US) Last Monday 14 Americans who were on the Diamond Princess Cruise-ship, (and tested positive for Covid-19), returned to the United States. The CDC (Center for Disease Control and Prevention) were opposed to their return but were overruled by officials at the U.S. State Department. None of the 14 returning travellers completed a 14-day quarantine. President Trump is furious.

(IRAQ) Iraq has its first case of the Coronavirus.

FEBRUARY 23
SUNDAY

(IRAN) In Iran 8 people have died of Covid-19. Schools, Universities and cultural centers in fourteen provinces have been shut down.

(IRAN) Afghanistan, Armenia, Turkey and Pakistan have closed their borders with Iran.

(ITALY) Three people have died in Italy. There are now 152 cases in the country. Three days ago Italy had 3 reported cases.

(JAPAN) The last passenger has left the Diamond Princess Cruise-ship. Hundreds of crewmembers are still on board. There are concerns that some passengers who tested negative and disembarked early could turn positive.

FEBRUARY 24
MONDAY

(GLOBAL) Stock Markets have plunged around the world after surges of Coronavirus cases in Italy and South Korea.

(CH) China has warned its citizens against travelling to the United States. This is due to Chinese tourists facing unfair treatment due to excessive prevention measures.

(ITALY) So far seven people have died in Italy.

(US) President Trump has tweeted that the Coronavirus is very much under control in the United States.

(AFGHANISTAN) Afghanistan has its first case of the Coronavirus.

(BAHRAIN) Bahrain has its first case of the Coronavirus.

(KUWAIT) Kuwait has its first case of the Coronavirus.

(OMAN) Oman has its first case of the Coronavirus.

FEBRUARY 25
TUESDAY

(GLOBAL) According to the WHO Situation Report #36

    The United States has 53 cases

    Finland has 1

    Germany has 16

    France has 12

    The UK has 13

    Sweden has 1

    Spain has 2

    Japan has 157

    South Korea has 977

    Singapore has 90

    Thailand has 37

    India has 3

    Canada has 10

    Iran has 61

    Australia has 22

    Denmark has 0

    Norway has 0

    The whole of South America has 0

    Portugal has 0

    The Pacific Islands have 0

    Apart from Egypt (which has 1) the whole of Africa has 0

    New Zealand has 0

(WHO) The World Health Organisation has announced that for the first time there are more cases outside of China than there is in China.

(IRAN) Iran's Deputy Health Minister, Iraj Harirchi, has tested positive for Coronavirus.

(ITALY) Italy is now the new focal point of the novel coronavirus outside of Asia. They now have 283 cases. 212 of these cases are in Lombardy. In an attempt to stop the virus from spreading Authorities have closed down 12 towns. So far 7 people have died.

(US) San Francisco has declared a State of Emergency. They are the first US city to do.

(ALGERIA) It's not reported in the WHO Situation Report above, (that although released today reports cases up to yesterday), but Algeria has its first case of the Coronavirus...

(AUSTRIA) Likewise, Austria has its first case of the Coronavirus.

(BRAZIL) And, Brazil has its first case of the Coronavirus.

(CROATIA) And also, Croatia has its first case of the Coronavirus.

(SWITZERLAND) And finally Switzerland records its first case of the Coronavirus.

FEBRUARY 26
WEDNESDAY

(WHO) The World Health Organisation Director-General has given a mission briefing on the WHO visit to Wuhan. 'The team has made a range of findings about the transmissibility of the virus, the severity of disease and the impact of the measures taken. They found that there is no significant change in the genetic makeup of the virus. They estimate that the measures taken by China have averted a significant number of cases. The key message that should give all countries hope, courage and confidence, is that this virus can be contained. The primary objective of all countries with cases must be to contain the virus. All countries must prepare for a potential pandemic. Every country needs to be ready to detect cases early, to isolate patients, trace contacts, provide quality clinical care, prevent hospital outbreaks, and prevent community transmission. There are three priorities:

First – All countries must prioritise protecting health workers.

Second – We must engage communities to protect people who are most at risk, particularly the elderly and people with underlying health conditions.

Third – We must protect countries that are most vulnerable by doing our utmost to contain epidemics in countries with the capacity to do it.'

(JAPAN) 705 people who were on the Diamond Princess have tested positive for Coronavirus. Four passengers have died.

(GEORGIA) Georgia has its first case of the Coronavirus.

(GREECE) Greece has its first case of the Coronavirus.

(NORTH MACEDONIA) North Macedonia has its first case of the Coronavirus.

(NORWAY) Norway has its first case of the Coronavirus.

(PAKISTAN) Pakistan has its first case of the Coronavirus.

(ROMANIA) Romania has its first case of the Coronavirus.

FEBRUARY 27
THURSDAY

(IRAQ) Yesterday Iraq banned all public gatherings. Today they have banned all travel to 9 countries: China; Iran; Japan; South Korea; Thailand; Singapore; Italy; Bahrain; and Kuwait.

(ITALY) There are 655 cases of Covid-19 in Italy now. Last Thursday they had recorded 3 cases.

(DENMARK) Denmark has its first case of the Coronavirus.

(ESTONIA) Estonia has its first case of the Coronavirus.

(NETHERLANDS) The Netherlands have reported their first case of the Coronavirus.

(SAN MARINO) San Marino has its first case of the Coronavirus.

FEBRUARY 28 FRIDAY

(NZ) COVID-19 IS IN NEW ZEALAND!

(NZ) New Zealand has reported its first case of Covid-19. The man recently visited Iran, flying back via Bali.

(SWITZERLAND) Switzerland has banned all gatherings over 1000 people until at least March 15th.

(AZERBAIJAN) Azerbaijan has its first case of the Coronavirus.

(BELARUS) Belarus has its first case of the Coronavirus.

(ICELAND) Iceland has its first case of the Coronavirus.

(LITHUANIA) Lithuania has its first case of the Coronavirus.

(MEXICO) Mexico has its first case of the Coronavirus.

(MONACO) Monaco has its first case of the Coronavirus.

(NIGERIA) Nigeria has its first case of the Coronavirus.

FEBRUARY 29
SATURDAY

(AUS) The bushfires in New South Wales have finally ended after 240 days. Although there is not much to celebrate in the world at the moment the end of the most devastating Australian bushfires ever recorded should be reason to celebrate something. The Australian bushfires blazed through over 42,000 square miles of land. This is almost the size of the entire North Island of New Zealand. 2000 homes were destroyed and 25 people lost their lives, 6 being Firefighters, (3 from New South Wales, three from the United States). It's estimated that a billion animals were killed.

(NZ) Because of the first New Zealand Covid-19 case, there has been a spate of 'panic buying' at Supermarkets in Auckland with queues running out the door and into the carpark.

(US) Washington State has declared a State of Emergency.

(ECUADOR) Ecuador has its first case of the Coronavirus.

(IRELAND) Ireland has its first case of the Coronavirus.

(LUXEMBOURG) Luxembourg has its first case of the Coronavirus.

(QATAR) Qatar has its first case of the Coronavirus.

(GLOBAL) The following 35 countries and territories reported their first cases in February: Algeria; Austria; Azerbaijan; Bahrain; Belarus; Belgium; Croatia; Denmark; Egypt; Ecuador; Estonia; Georgia; Greece; Iceland; Iran; Iraq; Ireland; Israel, Kuwait; Lebanon; Lithuania; Luxembourg; Mexico; Monaco; the Netherlands; New Zealand; Nigeria; North Macedonia; Norway; Oman; Pakistan; Qatar; Romania; San Marino; and Switzerland.

(GLOBAL) The above countries join the 27 countries that reported cases in January, (or earlier in the case of China): Australia; Cambodia; Canada; China; Finland; France; Germany; Hong Kong; India; Italy; Japan; Macau; Malaysia; Nepal; Philippines; Russia; Singapore; Spain; Sweden; South Korea; Sri Lanka; Taiwan; Thailand; the United Arab Emirates; the United Kingdom; the United States of America; and Vietnam.

FEBRUARY: IT ONLY TAKES AN AIRPORT TO INFECT A WORLD

In February I was starting to take a bit more notice of the virus because it was popping up in more and more countries around the world. Australia had reported its first case in late January so the virus was actually a lot closer to New Zealand than was comfortable. Australia is our closest neighbour. We're separated by 2000kms of water but thousands of Australians fly into the country everyday. I'd seen enough movies and read enough Stephen King to know that it only takes an airport to infect a world. People fly everywhere, and the airport is the greatest common denominator connecting countries.

So I saluted our Government's call to stop flights to and from China. To me it made absolute sense to stop these flights because China was the country where the virus had originated; and where it was still very much active. It can't have been an easy decision for the New Zealand Government knowing that the New Zealand economy would take a significant hit. But they did it.

My work colleagues and I discussed this, and much more, during our lunchtime sessions, and we wouldn't have been alone. All over New Zealand, and most certainly the world, people would have been discussing and debating this 'thing' out of China.

It sometimes helps to have an ex-veterinarian in the discussion group; it's probably less helpful to have someone versed in horror novels. Our diverse lunchtime discussions encompassed everything from border closures, to antibiotics, to the differences between virus's and bacteria, to hoaxes, vaccine development, regional lockdowns, civil war, immunity passports, and herd immunity, (this before we even knew that immunity passports and herd immunity had official names). We infected 50% of the world's population with the virus and did the maths. If 4% of those infected died then we predicted 160 million deaths worldwide. Ultimately we mutually agreed that closing the borders was probably a good thing if we wanted to save 200,000 New Zealanders.

But still, it was all just lunchtime talk. And towards the end of February New Zealand still didn't have any cases; and there was a good chance that we might get away with not seeing the virus at all... fingers crossed. After all, there were still a lot of countries without Covid-19. Most of Africa was free, as was South America. We might sneak through without seeing anything.

My optimism sort of sunk when Italy reported a surge in cases. That's when a switch sort of turned on and I realised that this thing was going to be HUGE. In my head, Italy was 'Modern;' a European country with a history that has influenced the world more than most others. Italy, with access to the latest medical knowledge and equipment, with State of the Art hospitals and support networks worldwide. Italy. How could it be floundering?

That woke me up. If Italy couldn't handle the Coronavirus, what chance did New Zealand have?

And then it was here.

Jason Komene 7 April, 2020

MARCH 2020

MARCH 1 SUNDAY

(GLOBAL) The Global death toll has passed 3000, (3050).

(GLOBAL) 45,122 people have recovered from the virus.

(AUS) Australia has had its first death from Covid-19. It was a person evacuated from the Diamond Princess Cruise-ship.

(US) Florida has declared a State of Emergency.

(US) Governor Andrew Cuomo has confirmed New York State's first case of Coronavirus. He says: 'There is no reason for undue anxiety, the general risk remains low in New York.'

(ARMENIA) Armenia has its first case of the Coronavirus.

(CZECH REPUBLIC) The Czech Republic has its first case of the Coronavirus.

(DOMINICAN REPUBLIC) The Dominican Republic has its first case of the Coronavirus.

(ST-BARTH) St-Barth has its first case of the Coronavirus.

(SAINT MARTIN) Saint Martin has its first case of the Coronavirus.

MARCH 2 MONDAY

(ITALY) A month ago there were 3 cases in Italy. Now there are 2036!

(US) Four residents of a nursing care facility in Seattle, Washington, have died.

(ANDORRA) Andorra has its first case of the Coronavirus.

(INDONESIA) Indonesia has its first case of the Coronavirus.

(JORDAN) Jordan has its first case of the Coronavirus.

(LATVIA) Latvia has its first case of the Coronavirus.

(MOROCCO) Morocco has its first case of the Coronavirus.

(PORTUGAL) Portugal has its first case of the Coronavirus.

(SAUDI ARABIA) Saudi Arabia has its first case of the Coronavirus.

(SENEGAL) Senegal has its first case of the Coronavirus.

(TUNISIA) Tunisia has its first case of the Coronavirus.

MARCH 3 TUESDAY

(AUS) Over the last few days there have been spates of panic buying in Australian Supermarkets. Many Supermarkets are selling out of Toilet Paper.

(ARGENTINA) Argentina has its first case of the Coronavirus.

(CHILE) Chile has its first case of the Coronavirus.

(GIBRALTAR) Gibraltar has its first case of the Coronavirus.

(LIECHTENSTEIN) Liechtenstein has its first case of the Coronavirus.

(UKRAINE) The Ukraine has its first case of the Coronavirus.

MARCH 4
WEDNESDAY

(C-19) SOCIAL DISTANCING. In its simplest form Social Distancing means keeping yourself away from other people; keeping your distance and out of reach of a sneeze. The recommended distance in New Zealand and many parts of the world is no closer than 2 meters (6 feet) from another person.

(AUS) A truck carrying toilet paper in Australia has crashed and burst into flames. The country has had bouts of toilet paper panic-buying over the last month.

(NZ) New Zealand has its second Covid-19 case. It's a 30 year-old woman returning from Italy via Singapore.

(US) California has declared a State of Emergency in response to the Coronavirus outbreak.

(FAROES) The Faroe Islands have their first case of the Coronavirus.

(HUNGARY) Hungary has its first case of the Coronavirus.

(POLAND) Poland has its first case of the Coronavirus.

(SLOVENIA) Slovenia has its first case of the Coronavirus.

MARCH 5 THURSDAY

(ITALY) There are 3858 cases of Coronavirus in Italy. Last Thursday they had 655 cases. The Thursday before… 3. Today's number is almost double what it was three days ago.

(NZ) New Zealand has recorded its third case. It's the first case of person-to-person transmission within New Zealand.

(NZ) There have been hostile social media attacks on the woman who tested positive yesterday. Her whole family are in isolation with her. Dr William Rainger of the Auckland Regional Public Health Service has said that: "They have become the focus of sustained and abusive bullying on social media and are being hounded by the media." The ARPHS are worried that such attacks will lead people to hide any illness that might be Covid-19.

(UK) The United Kingdom has reported its first two deaths. One is a lady in her 70's in Reading and the other is a man in his 80's in Milton Keynes.

(US) Maryland declares a State of Emergency.

(BOSNIA AND HERZEGOVINA) Bosnia and Herzegovina have their first case of the Coronavirus.

(COSTA RICA) Costa Rica has its first case of the Coronavirus.

(MARTINIQUE) Martinique has its first case of the Coronavirus.

(PALESTINE) Palestine has its first case of the Coronavirus.

(SOUTH AFRICA) South Africa has its first case of the Coronavirus.

MARCH 6 FRIDAY

(GLOBAL) The number of cases worldwide has hit 100,000. (102,052)

(NZ) New Zealand has recorded its fourth case. It is the partner of the 30 year-old lady who tested positive on March the 4th. On February 28 he attended a "Tool" Concert at Spark Arena. It's not known if he was contagious at the time but if so around 100 people may have been exposed to the virus.

(US) A State of Emergency has been declared in Indiana, Kentucky, Pennsylvania, and Utah.

(US) The South by Southwest (SXSW) 2020 festival, scheduled to run from March 13 to 22 has officially been cancelled due to the Coronavirus.

(BHUTAN) Bhutan has its first case of the Coronavirus.

(CAMEROON) Cameroon has its first case of the Coronavirus.

(COLOMBIA) Colombia has its first case of the Coronavirus.

(PERU) Peru has its first case of the Coronavirus.

(SERBIA) Serbia has its first case of the Coronavirus.

(SLOVAKIA) Slovakia has its first case of the Coronavirus.

(TOGO) Togo has its first case of the Coronavirus.

(VATICAN) The Vatican City has its first case of the Coronavirus.

MARCH 7 SATURDAY

(C-19) Some scientists believe that the virus may have originated in bats, passing to humans via an intermediary animal. The animal of choice seems to be the endangered Pangolin. The Pangolin is a scaly anteater-like animal that is the most illegally traded mammal in the world. It's prized for its meat and the claimed medicinal properties of its scales. In the early 2000's, Civet Cats became a scapegoat for the origin of SARS and were therefore hunted and killed mercilessly. There are concerns that the same thing will happen to the already endangered Pangolin.

(AUS) A doctor in Victoria has tested positive for Covid-19. He's in his 70's and had recently returned from the United States. From March 2 – 6 he saw about 70 patients at a Clinic in Melbourne and two patients at an aged-care facility. Patients are self-isolating.

(US) Since the first cases of Covid-19 were identified in January the United States have performed just 1583 tests, (there are 435 positive cases in the US), this despite President Trump having tweeted that "Anyone who wants a test, gets a test." Instead of using the test kits provided by the World Health Organisation the CDC created their own, sending them out in early February. Some of the test kits were faulty and produced inconclusive results. Hospitals were not permitted to do their own tests and had to send samples to one of a dozen testing labs, and then the results had to be certified by the CDC. This resulted in a bottleneck and ultimately delays. Tests were therefore restricted to those in close contact with a confirmed case, or those who had travelled from high-risk areas or countries, or those with a serious respiratory illness. The CDC say that they have now fixed the problems and the US will be able to test 75,000 people by the end of the week.

(US) New York State has declared a State of Emergency.

(BULGARIA) Bulgaria has its first case of the Coronavirus.

(FRENCH GUIANA) French Guiana has its first case of the Coronavirus.

(MALDIVES) The Maldives have their first case of the Coronavirus.

(MALTA) Malta has its first case of the Coronavirus.

(MOLDOVA) Moldova has its first case of the Coronavirus.

(PARAGUAY) Paraguay has its first case of the Coronavirus.

MARCH 8 SUNDAY

(AUS) There's a video circulating on YouTube showing three women fighting over toilet paper in an Australian supermarket. Two women have a trolley stacked with packets of toilet paper and another lady is asking if she can have just one pack. The two women with the rolls of toilet paper refuse and a brawl ensues. A shop assistant has to jump in and break it up. Even after the Police arrive the two women refuse to part with any toilet paper.

(US) Oregon has declared a State of Emergency.

(US) The number of cases in the United States has passed 500. There are 539 cases across 34 States. US expert on infectious diseases, Dr Anthony Fauci, says that it is possible that regional lockdowns could become necessary.

(ALBANIA) Albania has its first case of the Coronavirus.

(BANGLADESH) Bangladesh has its first case of the Coronavirus.

MARCH 9 MONDAY

(ISRAEL) Israel has imposed a 14-day quarantine for all International travellers.

(ITALY) Italy has extended its emergency Coronavirus measures to the entire country. People have been ordered to stay home and seek permission for essential travel. It is forbidden for people to gather in public.

(ITALY) Seven inmates have died during riots at prisons across Italy after authorities suspended all visits in an attempt to control the spread of Covid-19.

(US) States of Emergency have been declared in: Illinois; New Jersey; Ohio; and Rhode Island.

(BRUNEI) Brunei has its first case of the Coronavirus.

(BURKINA FASO) Burkina Faso has its first case of the Coronavirus.

(CHANNEL ISLANDS) The Channel Islands have their first case of the Coronavirus.

(CYPRUS) Cyprus has its first case of the Coronavirus.

MARCH 10 TUESDAY

(C-19) An animation by a New Zealand microbiologist (Siouxsie Wiles) and her friend has gone viral. It shows how to 'flatten the curve' of Covid-19 by using simple health measures: Wash Hands; Don't touch your face; If you're sick, stay home. It explains simply how flattening the curve eases the burden on the health system.

(ITALY) There are 10,149 cases of Covid-19 in Italy now. This is twice as many as it was five days ago.

(US) A State of Emergency has been declared in: Colorado; Massachusetts; Michigan; North Carolina; and Vermont.

(BOLIVIA) Bolivia has its first case of the Coronavirus.

(DR CONGO) The Democratic Republic of Congo has its first case of the Coronavirus.

(JAMAICA) Jamaica has its first case of the Coronavirus.

(MONGOLIA) Mongolia has its first case of the Coronavirus.

(PANAMA) Panama has its first case of the Coronavirus.

(TURKEY) Turkey has its first case of the Coronavirus.

MARCH 11
WEDNESDAY

(C-19) THE DIFFERENCE BETWEEN BACTERIA AND A VIRUS

The Bubonic Plague was Bacterial; Covid-19 is a Virus.

Bacteria are living single-cell organisms that do not need a host to survive.

1% of Bacteria cause disease. Most are beneficial to our health and the health of the earth.

Bacteria can only be seen under a microscope. They are gigantic compared to viruses.

Bacteria multiply by splitting in two. Each half grows and splits into two again. This repeats over and over.

Antibiotics can be used to treat some bacterial infections.

Notable examples of Bacterial diseases and epidemics are: the Bubonic Plague, Meningitis, Leprosy and Tuberculosis.

Viruses are not considered alive and need a host to survive long term. Without a host they are fragile and do not survive long.

Most viruses cause disease.

Viruses are smaller than cells.

The biggest virus is 10-100 times smaller than the tiniest Bacteria. Some viruses can even infect bacteria.

Viruses consist of one piece of genetic material (either DNA or RNA) and a protein shell called a capsid. A capsid might have protrusions used to bind to certain 'receptors' on a host cell. The 'receptors' can be used by the virus to de-

termine what type of hosts or host cell the virus can infect. Virus's survive and reproduce by 'hijacking' a cell and using its replicating properties to recreate itself.
Antibiotics will not work on viruses at all.

(US) States of Emergency have been declared in: Arizona; Arkansas; New Mexico; Louisiana; and Washington DC.

(US) 24 States have declared a State of Emergency due to the Coronavirus. Arizona; Arkansas; California; Colorado; Florida; Hawaii; Illinois; Indiana; Kentucky; Louisiana; Maryland; Massachusetts; Michigan; New Jersey; New Mexico; New York; North Carolina; Ohio; Oregon; Pennsylvania; Rhode Island; Utah; Vermont; Washington State.

(CUBA) Cuba has its first case of the Coronavirus.

(FRENCH POLYNESIA) French Polynesia has its first case of the Coronavirus.

(HONDURAS) Honduras has its first case of the Coronavirus.

(IVORY COAST) The Ivory Coast has its first case of the Coronavirus.

(RÉUNION) Réunion has its first case of the Coronavirus.

(ST VINCENT GRENADINES) St Vincent and the Grenadines have their first case of the Coronavirus.

MARCH 12 THURSDAY

(C-19) The World Health Organisation has declared that Covid-19 is a Pandemic. Europe has been placed as the centre of the Pandemic with more than 20,000 confirmed cases and almost 1000 deaths.

(GLOBAL) 20% of all students around the world are out of school because of the virus.

(AUS) Tom Hanks and his wife have both tested positive for Coronavirus. They are in Australia making an Elvis Presley film. There are now 120 confirmed cases in Australia.

(CANADA) Sophie Grégoire Trudeau, the wife of Canadian Prime Minister Justin Trudeau, has tested positive for Covid-19. The Prime Minister is going into self-isolation.

(FRANCE) From next Monday all nurseries, schools and universities will be closed in France.

(GREECE) Greece has closed theatres, gyms, cinemas, playgrounds, and entertainment centers for at least two weeks.

(IRAN) Iran's Deputy Health Minister, Iraj Harirchi, has recovered from Covid-19.

(ISRAEL) Israel has ordered the closure of all schools and universities.

(US) Tennessee and Virginia have declared a State of Emergency.

(US) New York officials have placed an indefinite ban on gatherings of more than 500 people. This means that Broadway Theatres in the city will have to close. The infection rate in New York State has tripled since Sunday. There are now nearly 100 cases of the virus. New York City has declared a State of Emergency.

(GHANA) Ghana has its first case of the Coronavirus.

(GUYANA) Guyana has its first case of the Coronavirus. (TRINIDAD AND TOBAGO) Trinidad and Tobago have their first case of the Coronavirus.

MARCH 13 FRIDAY

(GLOBAL) More than 5000 people have died of Covid-19. (5428).

(EUROPE) Denmark, Poland, and the Czech Republic have closed their borders.

(AUS) Formula 1 has cancelled the 2020 Australian Grand Prix after a member of the McLaren team tested positive for Covid-19.

(CH) Chinese Authorities have so far identified at least 266 people who were infected last year. According to Government Data the first case can be traced back to November 17, 2019.

(ITALY) There's an interview on New Zealand's Breakfast Television Show with a New Zealand lady stranded in Italy. She's in isolation and has heard that the medical centres and hospitals are running out of essential health resources and that the focus is being put on the young. The old are being shunted aside and forgotten.

(US) President Trump has declared a State of National Emergency. In his declaration he says that: '32 States, 3 Territories, 4 Tribes, and 1 Tribal Nation, spread geographically across our country, have declared a State of Emergency as a result of the virus.'

(US) The United States has suspended travel from all countries in Europe except the United Kingdom. The UK is exempt because it is not part of the Schengen border-free travel area. (The Schengen border-free travel area relates to 26 European countries that have abolished their internal borders to allow for the free and unrestricted movement of people - within common rules - between countries).

(GLOBAL) Eighteen countries today record their first cases

of Coronavirus!

(ANTIGUA AND BARBUDA) Antigua and Barbuda have their first case of the Coronavirus.

(ARUBA) Aruba has its first case of the Coronavirus.

(CAYMAN) The Cayman Islands have their first case of the Coronavirus.

(CURAÇAO) Curaçao has its first case of the Coronavirus.

(ETHIOPIA) Ethiopia has its first case of the Coronavirus.

(GABON) Gabon has its first case of the Coronavirus.

(GUADALUPE) Guadalupe has its first case of the Coronavirus.

(GUATEMALA) Guatemala has its first case of the Coronavirus.

(GUINEA) Guinea has its first case of the Coronavirus.

(KAZAKHSTAN) Kazakhstan has its first case of the Coronavirus.

(KENYA) Kenya has its first case of the Coronavirus.

(MAURITANIA) Mauritania has its first case of the Coronavirus.

(SAINT LUCIA) Saint Lucia has its first case of the Coronavirus.

(SUDAN) Sudan has its first case of the Coronavirus.

(SURINAME) Suriname has its first case of the Coronavirus.

(URUGUAY) Uruguay has its first case of the Coronavirus.

(VENEZUELA) Venezuela has its first case of the Coronavirus.

MARCH 14 SATURDAY

(GERMANY) Florian Reifschneider, from Germany, has started a "Stay The Fuck Home" campaign. The movement has taken off around the world via social media thanks to singers Taylor Swift and Ariana Grande jumping on board.

(NZ) A remembrance service for the 51 people killed in last year's Christchurch Mosque shootings has been cancelled due to concerns over the spread of Covid-19. Prime Minister Jacinda Ardern said that: 'We're saddened to cancel it but in remembering such a terrible tragedy we shouldn't create the risk of further harm being done.'

(NZ) From midnight tomorrow everyone coming into New Zealand (tourists as well as New Zealanders) must self-isolate for 14 days. Prime Minister Jacinda Ardern says: 'Alongside Israel, and a small number of Pacific Islands who have effectively closed their border, this decision will mean New Zealand will have the widest ranging and toughest border restrictions of any country in the world.' The travel restrictions will be reviewed at the end of March. Cruise ships have been asked to stay away until the end of June.

(NZ) Prime Minister Jacinda Ardern says that New Zealand has two choices as a Nation: 'One is to let Covid-19 roll on and simply to brace, the other is to go hard on measures to keep it out and stamp it out.' She adds that New Zealand: 'Can't stop a global pandemic from reaching us, but because it is in our power to slow it down I make no apology for choosing the second path. New Zealanders' public health comes first. If we have that we can recover from the impacts on the economy.'

(NZ) The sixth case of Covid-19 has been confirmed in New Zealand.

(US) The United States has over 2500 cases. Every State has reported cases except for West Virginia.

(US) All professional Sports Leagues in the United States have now suspended play. This includes the National Basketball Association, Major League Baseball, Major League Soccer and the National Hockey League.

(EQUATORIAL GUINEA) Equatorial Guinea has its first case of the Coronavirus.

(ESWATINI) Eswatini has its first case of the Coronavirus.

(MAYOTTE) Mayotte has its first case of the Coronavirus.

(NAMIBIA) Namibia has its first case of the Coronavirus.

(RWANDA) Rwanda has its first case of the Coronavirus.

(SEYCHELLES) The Seychelles have their first case of the Coronavirus.

MARCH 15 SUNDAY

(NZ) There are two more new cases today. One of them is an Australian guy who had symptoms in Australia, got tested, and flew to New Zealand before getting his results. He's now tested positive. There has been outrage over the man's senseless disregard for the health of others, considering the fact that he was sick enough to get tested but still travelled, no doubt coming into contact with people on the plane, at the airport, and who knows where else? New Zealand now has a total of 8 cases.

(NZ) There's a cruise ship called the Golden Princess in Akaroa harbour and no one is allowed to disembark. Three people are being held in isolation and one person has been tested.

(NZ) From midnight tonight every person entering New Zealand will have to self-isolate for 14 days. This includes any tourists planning to see the country. These are the tightest border restrictions of any country in the world.

(UK) The UK may consider a 'Herd Immunity' strategy where vulnerable people are isolated or quarantined while the rest of the public are left free to openly catch the virus, (therefore becoming immune to it). A British Political Strategist called Dominic Cummings is suspected to have suggested the same thing back in February, along with a comment that Herd Immunity will protect the Economy and... 'If that means some pensioners die, too bad.'

(US) Schools in New York City will close this week. The closures will affect 1.1 million children, 75,000 teachers and well over 1 million parents. Schools will be closed at least until April 20.

(US) President Trump has been tested for Covid-19. The test has come back negative.

(US) Maine and Oklahoma have declared a State of Emergency.

(BAHAMAS) The Bahamas have their first case of the Coronavirus.

(CAR) Central African Republic has its first case of the Coronavirus.

(CONGO) Congo has its first case of the Coronavirus.

(GUAM) Guam has its first case of the Coronavirus.

(UZBEKISTAN) Uzbekistan has its first case of the Coronavirus.

MARCH 16 MONDAY

(C-19) HOW COVID-19 ATTACKS

Covid-19 enters the body through the nose or throat. It finds a home in the lining of the nose, which is full of cells rich in a 'cell-surface receptor' called ACE2. ACE2 is critical to the body as it helps regulate processes like blood pressure, and wound healing. Unfortunately Covid-19 binds easily to ACE2 and stops it from performing its normal functions. It pretty much hitches a ride and the ACE2 receptor acts like a key unlocking access to a cell. Once inside the cell the virus hijacks the cell's machinery and makes heaps of copies of itself so that it can continue invading new cells.

As the virus is multiplying an infected person may be shedding copious amounts of it, especially during the first week or so, and, as it's in the nose, a cough or a sneeze can pass it easily onto others. The victim could show no symptoms at all, or they could develop a fever, a dry cough, a sore throat, loss of smell and taste, or have head and body aches. If the immune system doesn't beat it back during this initial phase, then the virus proceeds down the windpipe and attacks the lungs; and here it turns deadly.

The alveoli of the lungs are rich in ACE2 receptors for Covid-19 to bind to and take advantage of. Normally oxygen would be crossing these alveoli on its way to the rest of the body, but as the immune system is fighting at this location healthy oxygen transfer is disrupted. As the immune cells target and kill virus-infected cells a stew of fluid and dead cells, (pus), is left behind. This is the underlying pathology of pneumonia, causing coughing, fever, and shallow respiration.

Some patients can recover, but others deteriorate, developing Acute Respiratory Distress Syndrome (ARDS). Oxygen levels in their blood plummet as they struggle to breathe. These patients end up on ventilators. Many die. X-rays show lungs riddled with white opacities where black space (air) should be. Autopsies have shown alveoli stuffed with fluid: white blood cells, mucus and the detritus of destroyed lung cells.

(CH) The last two of Wuhan's temporary hospitals has been shut down due to the Coronavirus crisis improving in China. 16 temporary hospitals in Wuhan dealt with a total of 13,000 Covid-19 patients.

(NZ) The New Zealand Tourism Board has estimated that tourism in New Zealand is losing $650 million a week, with $10 Billion lost since the crisis began.

(NZ) Events featuring gatherings of 500 or more are to be cancelled in New Zealand, effective immediately.

(NZ) The cruise ship in Akaroa with suspected Covid-19 cases, the Golden Princess, has left Akaroa and is heading back to Melbourne. The one test that was performed has returned negative.

(US) There are over 4000 cases of Covid-19 in the US. (4611)

(US) Four days ago the Dow Jones Industrial Average dropped 2353 points, making it the worst single-day drop in history. Today it was even worse. The Dow fell 2997 points.

(BENIN) Benin has its first case of the Coronavirus.

(GREENLAND) Greenland has its first case of the Coronavirus.

(LIBERIA) Liberia has its first case of the Coronavirus.

(SOMALIA) Somalia has its first case of the Coronavirus.

(TANZANIA) Tanzania has its first case of the Coronavirus.

MARCH 17 TUESDAY

(GLOBAL) There are now 179,836 cases of Covid-19 in the world. 7098 people have died, and 78,324 people have recovered.

(C-19) TESTING FOR COVID-19

The two most common ways to test for Covid-19 is either a throat swab or a nasal swab. The throat swab is less invasive than the nasal swab but it's less sensitive to picking up a good result.

The person conducting the nasal swab inserts a long cotton-bud deep into your nose, and twirls it around for a few seconds. Here the cotton-bud collects a sample of secretions. The swab has to go pretty far back up the nose because to get a really good specimen cells and fluids must be collected along the entire passageway that connects the base of the nose to the back of the throat. This invasive procedure may cause the body to react in certain ways. It might bring tears to your eyes, or trigger a gag reflex. It will be uncomfortable but the discomfort disappears over time, some have said after about five minutes or so.

The sample then gets sent to a lab to see if the Covid-19 Coronavirus is present. The test is known as a nucleic acid amplification test, (NAAT). Using special reagents and fast temperature-switching equipment any RNA, (Ribonucleic Acid), present in the sample gets turned into DNA, (Deoxyribonucleic Acid), and if any of that RNA belonged to the Covid-19 Coronavirus then heaps of it gets duplicated: enough to be detected as a positive test. If none of the RNA belonged to the virus then there shouldn't be any detectable sign.

(CH) 3213 people have died in China of Covid-19.

(ITALY) 2158 have died in Italy.

(NZ) The Government has announced: 'The most significant peace-time economic plan in modern New Zealand history.' It involves a $12.1 billion relief package. $8.7 billion will go towards businesses and jobs. $2.8 billion for income support, and $500 million for health. Wage subsidies will be available immediately to businesses able to show a 30% decline in revenue compared with the same time last year. Employers will be paid $585.80 per week to cover each full time staff member, and $350 for part time staff, capped at $150,000 per business.

(NZ) Two visitors flaunting New Zealand's 14-day self-isolation rules are being deported.

(NZ) New Zealand has four new cases today, bringing the total to 12.

(US) West Virginia has reported its first Covid-19 case. The virus is now present in all 50 States of the United States.

(BARBADOS) Barbados has its first case of the Coronavirus.

(GAMBIA) Gambia has its first case of the Coronavirus.

(MONTENEGRO) Montenegro has its first case of the Coronavirus.

MARCH 18
WEDNESDAY

(EUROPE) Every European country has now closed their borders.

(CANADA/US) The United States and Canada have suspended non-essential travel between their two countries.

(ITALY) Italy has recorded the highest daily death toll so far; 475 deaths in one day. In one more day they could surpass China. Italy now has a total of 35,713 cases. A month ago they had 3 cases!

(NZ) The first community testing-centre for Covid-19 has opened in Christchurch. Five community based testing centres will open this weekend across the Auckland region.

(NZ) New Zealand has 8 new cases today; all of them related to overseas travel. There are now 20 cases in the country. All of them are in isolation.

(BERMUDA) Bermuda has its first case of the Coronavirus.

(DJIBOUTI) Djibouti has its first case of the Coronavirus.

(KYRGYZSTAN) Kyrgyzstan has its first case of the Coronavirus.

(MAURITIUS) Mauritius has its first case of the Coronavirus.

(MONTSERRAT) Montserrat has its first case of the Coronavirus.

(NEW CALEDONIA) New Caledonia has its first case of the Coronavirus.

(SINT MAATEN) Sint Maaten has its first case of the Coronavirus.

(ZAMBIA) Zambia has its first case of the Coronavirus.

MARCH 19 THURSDAY

(CH) For the first time since the crisis began China has recorded no new domestic cases. All of their new cases have been related to overseas travel.

(FRANCE) France has reported over 10,000 cases. (10,995).

(INDIA) India has banned all International incoming flights till March 28.

(MONACO) Prince Albert II of Monaco has tested positive for Covid-19. He is the first reigning Monarch or Head of State to announce contracting the virus.

(NZ) The New Zealand Government has called for every New Zealander that is still overseas to return home.

(NZ) The New Zealand Government has banned all groups of 100 people or more; except in Schools, Workplaces, Supermarkets, and Public Transport.

(NZ) New Zealand recorded another 8 cases today, bringing the total to 28.

(UK) On Friday every school in the United Kingdom will close.

(US) The United States now has more than 13,000 cases of Covid-19. (13,935). Ten days ago they had 704 cases.

(CHAD) Chad has its first case of the Coronavirus.

(EL SALVADOR) El Salvador has its first case of the Coronavirus.

(FIJI) Fiji has its first case of the Coronavirus.

(ISLE OF MAN) The Isle of Man has its first case of the Coronavirus.

(NICARAGUA) Nicaragua has its first case of the Coronavirus.

(NIGER) Niger has its first case of the Coronavirus.

MARCH 20 FRIDAY

(WHO) The World Health Organisation has distributed 1.5 million Covid-19 lab tests around the world; and they will need 80-100 times that amount.

(AUS) The Government has ramped up social distancing rules. Indoor gatherings of fewer than 100 people are still allowed but there must be at least 4 square metres for each person. Outdoor gatherings of 500 or more are banned.

(AUS) There's another cruise ship with Covid-19 issues. Three Australian passengers and one crewmember of the Ruby Princess cruise ship have tested positive. The ship left New Zealand five days ago after visiting five New Zealand ports.

(ITALY) The death toll in Italy is 3405, about 150 more than in China where the virus originated.

(NZ) New Zealand is now effectively sealed. It has closed its borders to all non-residents, and non-citizens. Australia has done likewise.

(NZ) There are 11 new cases in New Zealand.

(NZ) The Auckland Council has closed all pools, libraries, galleries, and other community facilities, for 14 days.

(NZ) Air New Zealand's shares have plummeted more than 40%. Covid-19 has hit Air New Zealand hard and they've warned that maybe 30% of their staff could be made redundant. The Government is lending the airline $900 million as a financial lifeline.

(US) There are more than 19,000 cases in the United States. (19,608).

(US) President Trump has boasted about the 'very encouraging results' of two drugs called chloroquine and hydroxychloroquine in the treatment of the novel coronavirus. The

US Food and Drug Administration have quickly said that these drugs have not been approved as treatments for Covid-19. Chloroquine and Hydroxychloroquine were developed in the 1940's as a treatment for malaria. Of the two, Hydroxychloroquine is less toxic.

(US) President Trump has issued an executive order invoking the Defence Production Act to battle the Covid-19 pandemic. The Defence Production Act permits the Federal Government to impose some control over private-sector industries to ensure the production of material that is deemed necessary for National Defence. In this case: Ventilators; Testing kits; Protective masks; Gloves; and Gowns.

(ANGOLA) Angola has its first case of the Coronavirus.

(CABO VERDE) Cabo Verde has its first case of the Coronavirus.

(HAITI) Haiti has its first case of the Coronavirus.

(MADAGASCAR) Madagascar has its first case of the Coronavirus.

(PAPUA NEW GUINEA) Papua New Guinea has its first case of the Coronavirus.

(ZIMBABWE) Zimbabwe has its first case of the Coronavirus.

MARCH 21 SATURDAY

(AUS) Thousands have flocked to Sydney's Bondi Beach defying social distancing orders brought about to prevent the spread of the Coronavirus. Groups of more than 500 are not permitted to congregate outside.

(EGYPT) Egypt has ordered all mosques and churches to shut their doors to worshippers for 14 days. There are more than 100,000 mosques in Egypt.

(NZ) New Zealand has implemented a 4 level alert system.

- Alert Level 1 – (Prepare – where the disease is contained).

  Risk Assessment based on: Heightened risk of importing Covid-19 or sporadic imported cases or isolated household transmission associated with imported cases.

- Alert Level 2 (Reduce – where disease is contained but risks of community transmission are growing).

  Assessed on the high risk of importing Covid-19, increase in imported cases or household transmission, or a single isolated cluster outbreak.

- Alert Level 3 (Restrict – where there's a heightened risk that the disease is not contained).

  Assessment based on community transmission occurring or multiple clusters breaking out.

- Alert Level 4 (Eliminate – the disease is not contained).

  Risk assessment based on sustained and intensive transmission and widespread outbreaks.

(NZ) New Zealand has been placed immediately into Alert Level 2.

(NZ) No matter the threat level essential shops like Supermarkets and Pharmacies will remain open.

(ERITREA) Eritrea has its first case of the Coronavirus.

(TIMOR-LESTE) Timor-Leste has its first case of the Coronavirus.

(UGANDA) Uganda has its first case of the Coronavirus.

MARCH 22 SUNDAY

(GLOBAL) The number of Coronavirus cases around the world has doubled in a week. There are nearly 300,000 cases worldwide.

(GLOBAL) The International Olympic Committee is still pressing on with plans to hold the 2020 Olympics in Tokyo, (July 24 to August 9), despite Europe and the UK struggling to control Covid-19.

(GERMANY) Chancellor Angela Merkel has gone into isolation because her doctor has tested positive for the Coronavirus.

(GERMANY) Germany has banned groups of more than 2; except for families. These restrictions will be in place for at least 2 weeks.

(UK) Teddy Bears have begun to appear in London windows. The idea sprang up on Facebook inspired by the Michael Rosen children's book: "We're Going On A Bear Hunt." The idea is to brighten the spirits of children as they hunt for bears during their daily exercise walks during Lockdown.

(US) The number of cases in the United States has shot up to 33,946. It has almost gone up ten times since last Sunday's 3622 cases.

(GRENADA) Grenada has its first case of the Coronavirus.

(MOZAMBIQUE) Mozambique has its first case of the Coronavirus.

(SYRIA) Syria has its first case of the Coronavirus.

MARCH 23 MONDAY

(GLOBAL) Canada, Australia and Great Britain have said that they will pull out of this year's Olympics in Tokyo if they are not postponed for a year.

(AUS) The NRL (Australia's National Rugby League club competition) has suspended the 2020 season indefinitely for the first time in its history.

(NZ) Because New Zealand is at Alert Level 2 people over 70 are being asked to stay home.

(NZ) At 1:40 PM New Zealand went to Alert Level 3 (two days after Alert Level 2). The country will go to Alert Level 4 in two days. Schools, Universities and childcare centres will be closed from tomorrow. All non-essential businesses/services must shut in 48 hours. New Zealanders should stay home unless visiting an essential service. Supermarkets, pharmacies, and service stations will remain open.

(NZ) In regards to the Level 4 Lockdown coming up in two days Prime Minister Jacinda Ardern has said that: 'the best approach is to "go hard and go early" to combat the spread of Covid-19. These are major measures, but they are necessary to give us the best chance in our fight against the spread of the virus. We know that things will get worse before they get better. In the short term, case numbers will rise, but that doesn't mean that self-isolation measures aren't working.'

(BELIZE) Belize has its first case of the Coronavirus.

(MYANMAR) Myanmar has its first case of the Coronavirus.

(TURKS AND CAICOS) The Turks and Caicos Islands have their first case of the Coronavirus.

MARCH 24 TUESDAY

(GLOBAL) The number of worldwide cases has more than doubled since this time last week. There are now 422,907 cases, out of which 19,193 people have died. 108,930 people have recovered.

(GLOBAL) The International Olympic Committee and the Tokyo Organising Committee have announced that the 2020 Summer Olympics and Paralympics are going to be re-scheduled for a date beyond 2020, but no later than Summer 2021.

(AUS) Australia has banned all overseas travel. They have also put restrictions on gatherings. No more than 5 people may attend a wedding and no more than 10 people may attend a funeral.

(NZ) Grant Robertson, the Finance Minister, has announced that the Government is negotiating with banks to ensure that nobody loses their home as a result of defaulting on mortgage payments during the pandemic.

(NZ) Teddy Bears have started turning up in New Zealand windows under a "We're Not Scared" banner.

(NZ) New Zealand has 40 new cases taking the total to 155. The good news is that 12 people have recovered in New Zealand.

(UK) Britain is in lockdown for 3 weeks. Public gatherings of more than 2 people are banned.

(US) Chinese-Americans and other Asian-Americans are contending with growing racism in the form of verbal and physical assaults. Gun owners are seeing a surge of first-time Chinese-Americans buying guns to protect themselves.

(LAOS) Laos has its first case of the Coronavirus.

(LIBYA) Libya has its first case of the Coronavirus.

MARCH 25
WEDNESDAY

(NZ) There are 50 new cases in New Zealand today. This brings the total number of cases to 205. Of this total 22 people have fully recovered.

(NZ) New Zealand will quarantine up to 10,000 returning Kiwis from abroad. The country can expect to have several thousand more cases of Covid-19 before strict self-isolation of the whole population has an effect on transmission.

(NZ) The Leader of the Opposition, Simon Bridges, is to chair a cross-party committee that will scrutinise the Government's response to Covid-19. Two thirds of the Committee will come from opposition parties (National and ACT) and the remainder will come from Governing Parties (Labour, New Zealand First, and the Greens).

(NZ) Jacinda Ardern, the NZ Prime Minister, says that we must all act like we've got Covid-19, and think about the impact we'll have on others if we go out unnecessarily. She adds that: 'we might not be at work, but we all have a job. Our job is to save lives.'

(NZ) A State Of Emergency has been declared. The Government can now control fuel and food supplies, cordon off towns and cities, and prevent air travel.

(NZ) At 6:30 PM cell phones all over New Zealand started shrieking an emergency alarm. It was a message from Civil Defence that read:

This message is for all of New Zealand.

We are depending on you. Follow the rules and STAY

HOME. Act as if you have Covid-19. This will save lives. Remember:
-    Where you stay tonight is where YOU MUST stay from now on
-    You must only be in physical contact with those you are living with.
It is likely level 4 measures will stay in place for a number of weeks.
Let's all do our bit to unite against Covid-19.
Kia Kaha

(NZ) 11:59 PM. New Zealand is in Lockdown.

(GUINEA-BISSAU) Guinea-Bissau has its first case of the Coronavirus.

(MALI) Mali has its first case of the Coronavirus.

(SAINT KITTS AND NEVIS) Saint Kitts and Nevis have their first case of the Coronavirus.

(BRITISH VIRGIN ISLANDS) The British Virgin Islands have their first case of the Coronavirus.

MARCH 26 THURSDAY

(GLOBAL) As well as Tom Hanks, some other celebrities have contracted the virus too. Idris Elba, Olga Kurylenko, Kristofer Hivju, Daniel Day Kim, Placido Domingo, and Jackson Browne.

(GLOBAL) Having first started in Italy and Spain during their lockdowns, many citizens are coming together (from the safety of their homes) to applaud the health workers at the forefront of the fight against Covid-19. Applause has now been extended to all essential workers.

(C-19) BUBBLE.

New Zealanders have been told to stay in their 'bubble.' A 'bubble' refers to the people you share your household with. They could be flatmates, parents, siblings, children, partners; whoever was under your roof when Lockdown was imposed. Your bubble is exclusive to you and your group; NO ONE ELSE! And you must not invade someone else's bubble. To do so you not only endanger the people in their bubble but you jeopardise your own group too when you return to your bubble. Siouxsie Wiles has a simple animation of a man 'popping' over to see his elderly parents, effectively 'popping' both his own bubble as he leaves home, and his parent's bubble when he enters their home.

(NZ) New Zealand is now at Alert Level 4. This means that everyone must stay home unless they work for what is deemed an essential business or service. People may go out for essential needs, (groceries, petrol, medicine etc.).

(NZ) There are 78 new cases in New Zealand today. This brings the total to 283 cases. 27 people have recovered from the virus. There have been a total of 12,683 tests carried out in

New Zealand.

(UK) Prince Charles has tested positive for Covid-19.

(US) The United States now has the most confirmed active cases in the world, surpassing China and Italy. They rank 6th in the total number of deaths.

(US) New York City has become the epicentre of the Covid-19 crisis in the US. They have recorded over 25,000 cases.

(ANGUILLA) Anguilla has its first case of the Coronavirus.

MARCH 27 FRIDAY

(GLOBAL) The number of confirmed cases in the world has passed half a million. There are 558,500 confirmed cases. 128,000 people have recovered. 25,251 people have died.

(CH) A Chinese lady called Wei Guixan was the first person to test positive for the virus. She sold live shrimps at the Wuhan market and believes she became infected after using a toilet shared with wild meat sellers.

(ITALY) Italy has had the highest single day death toll for any country: 919.

(NZ) The second day of Lockdown, Alert Level 4.

(NZ) There are 368 cases of the virus in New Zealand now. A week ago the country had 39. Eight people are in hospital, with two in a less than stable condition.

MARCH 28 SATURDAY

(CANADA) Prime Minister Justin Trudeau's wife, Sophie Grégoire Trudeau, has recovered from Covid-19. She and the Prime Minister have been self-isolating with their family since the 12th of March. The Prime Minister has been giving daily news conferences from outside of his home.

(NZ) The third day of Lockdown, Alert Level 4.

(NZ) There are 83 new cases in New Zealand. The country now has a total of 451 cases. Eight Air New Zealand staff have tested positive. So far 50 people have recovered from the virus. There are 12 people in hospital.

(NZ) There have been more cases of abuse surfacing on social media, all aimed at people who have contracted the disease.

(SPAIN) 832 people have died today in Spain. They have a total of 5690 fatalities.

(UK) Prime Minister Boris Johnson has tested positive for the virus. He's been meeting lots of people and blatantly shaking their hands. Boris Johnson is the highest profile political leader to have contracted the virus.

(US) President Trump says he is considering quarantining New York, New Jersey and Connecticut.

MARCH 29 SUNDAY

(CH) The situation has calmed a bit in China. Some of the restrictions people have been living under have been lifted, with some travel restrictions being loosened in Wuhan.

(NZ) The fourth day of Lockdown, Alert Level 4.

(NZ) New Zealand has had its first Covid-19 death.

(NZ) New Zealand has 63 new cases today, bringing the total to 514.

(NZ) The New Zealand Police have received over 1000 phone calls reporting possible breaches of the Lockdown. They now have a dedicated website to report such breaches.

(US) The United States have reported 145,526 cases. Two weeks ago they had 3622 cases.

(US) In the United States the first baby to die of Covid-19 has been reported.

(US) President Trump has backed down and decided not to quarantine New York, New Jersey and Connecticut.

(US) More people have died in New York (672) than the Netherlands (639), Germany (433) or Belgium (353). The US has more cases than anyone. 124,217. Italy has 92,472, and China has 82,009.

MARCH 30 MONDAY

(NZ) The fifth day of Lockdown, Alert Level 4.

(NZ) Anne Guenole, 74 years old, was the first lady to die in New Zealand of Covid-19. She fell ill on March 21. The next day she developed diarrhoea. By Wednesday she had aches and a fever and went into hospital. She was tested on Wednesday, confirmed positive on Saturday and died on Sunday.

(NZ) There are 75 new cases in New Zealand. The country now has 589 cases of Covid-19.

(US) Studies into the effectiveness of hydroxychloroquine in the prevention of Covid-19 are about to take place in New York and Washington State. Plans are to enrol 2000 participants who are close contacts of people with Covid-19. Participants will be randomly assigned hydroxychloroquine or a placebo for two weeks. The trial is expected to last eight weeks with results hopefully available by the US summer.

(BOTSWANA) Botswana has its first case of the Coronavirus.

MARCH 31 TUESDAY

(AUS) 440 Passengers of the Ruby Princess Cruise-ship have tested positive for Covid-19. As of today 5 passengers have died.

(MONACO) The reigning Monarch of Monaco, Prince Albert II, has recovered from Covid-19.

(NZ) The sixth day of Lockdown, Alert Level 4.

(NZ) There are 14 significant clusters in New Zealand. The largest is Marist College in Auckland which has 48 cases associated with it so far.

1. Marist College (48 cases)
2. World Hereford Conference (24 cases)
3. The Redoubt Bar in Matamata (23 cases)
4. A Wellington travel group (to USA) (16 cases)
5. A Hamilton Rest Home (14 cases)
6. A Wellington Wedding (11 cases)
7. A Blenheim Sports team visit (to USA) (9 cases)
8. A Christchurch business (8 cases)
9. A Bluff Wedding (8 cases)
10. A local Organisation in Marlborough (6 cases)
11. A local business in Auckland (4 cases)
12. A cluster in Auckland (4 cases)
13. A cluster in Hutt City (4 cases)
14. Another cluster in Hutt City (4 cases)

(NZ) There are 58 new cases in New Zealand today. The total is now 647.

(NZ) The State Of Emergency in NZ has been extended by seven days.

(US) Roughly 80% of all Americans are under Lockdown as

35 States issue stay at home orders.

(US) Government Scientists estimate that the Covid-19 pandemic could kill 100,000 to 240,000 Americans.

(BURUNDI) Burundi has its first case of the Coronavirus.

(SIERRA LEONE) Sierra Leone has its first case of the Coronavirus.

(GLOBAL) The following 138 countries and territories reported their first cases in March: Albania; Andorra; Angola; Anguilla; Antigua and Barbuda; Argentina; Armenia; Aruba; Bahamas; Bangladesh; Barbados; Belize; Benin; Bermuda; Bhutan; Bolivia; Bosnia and Herzegovina; Botswana; British Virgin Islands; Brunei; Bulgaria; Burkina Faso; Burundi; Cabo Verde; Cameroon; Cayman Islands; Central African Republic; Chad; Channel Islands; Chile; Colombia; Congo; Costa Rica; Cuba; Curaçao; Cyprus; Czech Republic; DR Congo; Djibouti; Dominican Republic; El Salvador; Equatorial Guinea; Eritrea; Eswatini; Ethiopia; Faroe Islands; Fiji; French Guinea; French Polynesia; Gabon; Gambia; Ghana; Gibraltar; Greenland; Grenada; Guadalupe; Guam; Guatemala; Guinea; Guinea-Bissau; Guyana; Haiti; Honduras; Hungary; Indonesia; Isle Of Man; Ivory Coast; Jamaica; Jordan; Kazakhstan; Kenya; Kyrgyzstan; Laos; Latvia; Liberia; Libya; Liechtenstein; Madagascar; Maldives; Mali; Malta; Martinique; Mauritania; Mauritius; Mayotte; Moldova; Mongolia; Montenegro; Montserrat; Morocco; Mozambique; Myanmar; Namibia; New Caledonia; Nicaragua; Niger; Palestine; Panama; Papua New Guinea; Paraguay; Peru; Poland; Portugal; Réunion; Rwanda; Saudi Arabia; St Barth; Saint Kitts and Nevis; Saint Lucia; Saint Martin; St Vincent and the Grenadines; Senegal; Serbia; Seychelles; Sierra Leone; Sint Maaten; Slovakia; Slovenia; Somalia; South Africa; Sudan; Suriname; Syria; Tanzania; Timor-Leste; Togo; Trinidad and Tobago; Tunisia; Turkey; Turks and Caicos Islands; Uganda; Ukraine; Uruguay; Uzbekistan; Vatican City; Venezuela; Zambia; and Zimbabwe.

(GLOBAL) The following 35 countries and territories reported their first cases in February: Algeria; Austria; Azerbaijan; Bahrain; Belarus; Belgium; Croatia; Denmark; Egypt; Ecuador; Estonia; Georgia; Greece; Iceland; Iran; Iraq; Ireland; Israel, Kuwait; Lebanon; Lithuania; Luxembourg; Mexico; Monaco; the Netherlands; New Zealand; Nigeria; North Macedonia; Norway; Oman; Pakistan; Qatar; Romania; San Marino; and Switzerland.

(GLOBAL) The following 27 countries and territories reported their first cases in January, (or earlier in the case of China): Australia; Cambodia; Canada; China; Finland; France; Germany; Hong Kong; India; Italy; Japan; Macau; Malaysia; Nepal; Philippines; Russia; Singapore; Spain; Sweden; South Korea; Sri Lanka; Taiwan; Thailand; the United Arab Emirates; the United Kingdom; the United States of America; and Vietnam.

(GLOBAL) More than a third of humanity is under some form of Lockdown.

MARCH: IT'S NOT ROCKET SCIENCE

I could see Lockdown coming.

I think all of us could. It was happening all over the world so it was only a matter of time before New Zealand followed suit. We were already recording cases in the community so it was pretty obvious that to prevent further spread of the virus we'd have to restrict our movements. Some people I knew had already taken it upon themselves to self-isolate, stocking up on groceries and locking their doors to everyone outside of their household 'bubble.' They were being cautious, but unless the whole country joined them then their self-imposed isolation was apt to be a very very long one or would just collapse over time. The sooner everyone got into Lockdown mode then the quicker we could get rid of this virus for good. And if the maths was right then this thing could be over with in a month or so.

According to what we already knew about the virus it took up to two weeks for Covid-19 to manifest itself and for people to start showing symptoms. So you didn't have to be a rocket scientist to understand that in the first two weeks of Lockdown, if everyone stuck religiously to their bubble with absolutely no outside contacts at all, then the virus would reveal itself if it was present. And if it did appear it would be trapped inside that bubble with nowhere to go. The virus would be contained.

If the virus didn't manifest itself inside your bubble during those first two weeks, then the people in your bubble could almost be considered Covid-free. But you would still need to do another two weeks isolation. Why? Because someone in your bubble could be asymptomatic! Not everyone shows symptoms. A second incubation period would give more opportunity for the virus to show.

Even if no one was asymptomatic and everyone in your bubble was Covid-free you would still need to isolate for that second fortnight because studies have shown that mild cases of the virus take up to two weeks to recover. So you have to give those infected bubbles out there, scattered around New Zealand, a chance to get well.

So, okay, four weeks has gone by, (two incubation periods) and your family is driving you crazy and your bubble is Covid-free and you just need to get out, but you're still waiting. Can you leave your bubble yet?

Maybe? It will depend on any continuing cases occurring in those infected bubbles out there. One person in the bubble might be infected, and then another might catch it five days later. Every time someone within a bubble catches the virus the two-week recovery clock would need to be reset. Depending on the number of people in the bubble this could go on for months, with people passing the virus on to bubble members like a relay baton. Whether it's safe to leave Lockdown or not will most likely be determined by the people monitoring all those infected bubbles.

So that's the maths. Like I said, it's not rocket science but it looks like two incubation periods should be enough to get rid of most of the virus. Add a few more incubation periods for safety and the thing should be gone. On paper it looks good, but in reality it will probably take longer, and not just because of continuing cases within bubbles.

Why could it take longer? Because people are involved; and people are unpredictable. No one knows what people are capable of until they do it. We know that some of them can't even wash their hands, so how do you think they'll handle Lockdown?

One thing we can be sure of though. The longer people mess

it up the longer the virus will be in the community and the longer we will be in Lockdown.

Covid-19 doesn't play fair, but without us it would be nothing.

Jason Komene 9 April 2020

APRIL 2020

APRIL 1 WEDNESDAY

(GLOBAL) There are over 870,000 confirmed cases of the virus around the world. 43,000 people have died. 194,191 people have recovered.

(GLOBAL) Due to many cities being under Lockdown, and the streets being free of traffic and people, there have been signs of wild animals venturing into towns and cities. Wild Goats are walking the streets of Llandudno in Wales, while Coyotes have visited San Francisco.

(NZ) The seventh day of Lockdown, Alert Level 4.

(NZ) The majority of the Covid-19 cases in New Zealand fit within the 20-29 year-old age group. They make up 183 of the 708 cases in New Zealand. Prime Minister Jacinda Ardern has blasted out at them, saying that while they might not be in as much danger as older people they are currently acting as the main vector of transmission in New Zealand.

(NZ) There are 61 new cases today. New Zealand has a total of 708 cases. A week ago there were 205. Two weeks ago: 20.

(SPAIN) Spain has had over 100,000 Coronavirus cases. More than 9000 people have died. This is the second highest number of Covid-19 deaths after Italy.

(UK) The Wimbledon Tennis Competition has been cancelled for the first time since World War Two. Wimbledon had been scheduled to run from June 29 to July 12. Roger Federer has tweeted that he's: 'devastated.'

(CARIBBEAN NETHERLANDS) The Caribbean Netherlands have their first case of the Coronavirus.

APRIL 2 THURSDAY

(GLOBAL) There are now 1 million cases of Covid-19. Sixteen days ago there were 179,836 cases.

(NZ) The eighth day of Lockdown, Alert Level 4.

(NZ) The Chatham Islands are in Lockdown but panic-buying on the New Zealand mainland has put pressure on their supply chain. Because of their isolation the Chathams usually buy in bulk. All the basic staples that the Chathams need are what New Zealand is buying up large.

(NZ) There are 89 new cases in New Zealand. This brings the total to 797. Of these 92 people have recovered. Thirteen people are in a stable condition in hospital.

(PERU) Men and women will be allowed to leave their homes on different days in an attempt to slow the spread of Covid-19 in Peru, and limit the number of people in public. Men will be able to go for essential supplies on Mondays, Wednesdays and Fridays. Women on Tuesdays, Thursdays and Saturdays. No one will be allowed out on Sundays.

(MALAWI) Malawi has its first case of the Coronavirus.

APRIL 3 FRIDAY

(ECUADOR) Hospitals in Guayaquil have quickly been overwhelmed as the Covid-19 virus rages through Ecuador. Mortuary workers can't, or wont, collect dead bodies. Some bodies have been left outside in the tropical heat for days waiting for collection.

(GERMANY) After almost two weeks in self-isolation German Chancellor Angela Merkel has returned to her Berlin office. She tested negative for the Coronavirus several times.

(NZ) The ninth day of Lockdown, Alert Level 4.

(NZ) New Zealand has 71 new cases bringing the total to 868.

(UK) A UK company is working on an Antibody test kit that determines if people have previously been exposed to Covid-19. It's a finger prick test similar to HIV. The test determines if someone has built up immunity to Covid-19. If they have then they've already had Covid-19, perhaps without even knowing it.

(US) A San Francisco company is working with Antibodies that block and stop SARS. Covid-19 is a cousin of SARS. They've mutated the Antibodies slightly and now they bind onto Covid-19 and block the spot where the virus gains entry into a cell. It will act like an Anti-viral and can be given to people who are sick. Within 20 minutes their body will be flooded with antibodies sticking to Covid-19. The disadvantage compared to a vaccine is that a vaccine gives a year or more of protection. The Antibodies would only give protection for 8 to 10 weeks. The US military will test the antibodies in their lab (against actual Covid-19), and another lab will start tests to make sure the medicine is safe for humans. If it's good then they may be able to release it under what is called 'compassionate use' (avoiding all the regulations etc.). It could be out there by early September.

(US) 6.6 Million Americans filed for unemployment benefits last week. The week before saw 3.28 million claims.

(US) The United States had over 32,000 cases today.

(US) President Trump has signed an order to stop N-95 facemasks and other Personal Protective equipment from being exported to other countries.

(FALKLANDS) The Falkland Islands have their first case of the Coronavirus.

APRIL 4 SATURDAY

(GLOBAL) As millions have been forced to stay at home many people and businesses have turned to Video Conferencing Services to keep in touch with each other. The most popular app is called Zoom. There were up to 200 million daily users in March.

(NZ) The tenth day of Lockdown, Alert Level 4.

(NZ) Today there are 82 new cases bringing the New Zealand total to 950. The New Zealand Health Director-General, Ashley Bloomfield, says we might be seeing the peak of infections as the number of new cases is flattening off as testing is increased.

(TURKEY) All public gatherings have been banned and people are only allowed to leave their homes on essential trips for food or medicine.

(WESTERN SAHARA) The Western Sahara has its first case of the Coronavirus.

APRIL 5 SUNDAY

(EUROPE) Spain has passed out Italy as the country with the most cases in Europe. They have 131,646 cases compared to Italy's 128,948.

(NZ) The eleventh day of Lockdown, Alert Level 4.

(NZ) A man has been arrested in New Zealand for deliberately sneezing over shoppers at the Fresh Choice Supermarket in Barrington, Christchurch. He filmed himself doing it and uploaded the video to Facebook.

(NZ) The New Zealand Health Minister, David Clark, has been seen going for a Mountain-bike ride during Lockdown; thus ignoring the Lockdown advice given by the Prime Minister. He admits that now is not the time to engage in higher risk activities.

(NZ) New Zealand has passed 1000 cases of Covid-19. There are 89 new cases today and the total is now 1039. 156 of these cases have recovered. 74% of the cases are Pakeha (Caucasian), 8.3% Asian, 7.6% Maori and 3.3% Pasifika.

(URUGUAY) There's another cruise ship struck by Covid-19. The Greg Mortimer is currently held in Uruguayan waters. There are 16 New Zealanders on board. They've been confined to their cabins since March 22nd. 128 of the 217 passengers and crew have tested positive for Covid-19.

(US) The United States has almost three times as many cases as Spain with 336,673 cases. New York is the worst hit state with 123,018 cases. New Jersey is second with 37,505. Michigan is third with 15,718.

(US) A tiger at the Bronx Zoo in New York City has tested positive for Covid-19. It's the first known case of an animal getting sick from human-to-animal transmission.

(SAINT PIERRE AND MIQUELON) Saint Pierre and Miquelon have their first case of the Coronavirus.

(SOUTH SUDAN) South Sudan has its first case of the Coronavirus.

APRIL 6 MONDAY

(AUS) On March 19, 2700 passengers got off the Ruby Princess Cruise ship in Sydney. 600 of the passengers and crew have since tested positive and 11 people have died. A Class Action is being prepared by lawyers against the Ruby Princess operators for failing to protect its passengers.

(IRAN) Iran has 60,000 cases, the highest number of cases in the Middle East.

(NZ) The twelfth day of Lockdown, Alert Level 4.

(NZ) There are 22,000 New Zealanders stranded overseas. The Government has organised a mercy flight to rescue New Zealanders stranded in Peru.

(NZ) To alleviate worries amongst New Zealand's younger population Prime Minister Jacinda Ardern has classified the Tooth Fairy and the Easter Bunny as essential workers. She says that because it's a difficult time the Easter Bunny might not be able to get everywhere this year.

(NZ) There are 67 new cases today. The total is 1106. Out of that 176 have recovered.

(UK) Queen Elizabeth II has delivered a speech to the Commonwealth. She has only done this sort of thing three times before; (the Queen Mother's death in 2002, Lady Diana's death in 1997, and the first Gulf War in 1991). She acknowledged that many families are suffering and thanked the National Health Service and those in essential jobs. She also thanked those staying home.

(UK) UK Prime Minister Boris Johnson has been hospitalised after 10 days battling Covid-19.

(US) The death toll in the United States has passed 10,000.

(SAO TOME AND PRINCIPE) Sao Tome and Principe have

their first case of the Coronavirus.

APRIL 7 TUESDAY

(ANTARTICA) Antarctica is the only continent not touched by Covid-19.

(NZ) The thirteenth day of Lockdown, Alert Level 4.

(NZ) David Clark, the NZ Health Minister who went mountain-biking during Lockdown, has admitted to taking his family to the beach during the Weekend of the Lockdown. The beach was 20km away from his home. Prime Minister Jacinda Ardern says that she would have sacked him if not for the Covid-19 pandemic and the disruption it would make getting a new Health Minister up to speed. Instead he's been demoted to the bottom of the Labour Party's Cabinet List and lost his ministerial role as Associate Finance Minister.

(NZ) Air New Zealand is considering laying off 387 pilots as part of its cutback measures.

(NZ) There are 54 new cases of Covid-19 in New Zealand. The total is now 1160 cases. 65 people have recovered. This is the first day in New Zealand that recoveries have exceeded new cases.

(UK) Boris Johnson has been moved to Intensive Care after his coronavirus symptoms worsened.

(UK) JK Rowling has revealed that she experienced all the symptoms of coronavirus but has recovered. She wasn't actually tested though. She has endorsed a respiratory breathing technique that she says helped her.

APRIL 8 WEDNESDAY

(GLOBAL) Pollution levels have plummeted due to Lockdowns trapping billions of people at home. In India, where air pollution is amongst the worst in the world, people are reporting seeing the Himalayas for the first time.

(CH) After more than 10 weeks the Lockdown in Wuhan, the city where Covid-19 first emerged, has been lifted.

(NZ) The fourteenth day of Lockdown, Alert Level 4.

(NZ) 120 Covid-19 testing centres are now operating in New Zealand. The testing centres come in a range of set-ups. They could be a Portacom, tent, GP Clinic, or a drive-thru.

(NZ) The Government is discussing the possibility of using a Mobile Phone App for contact tracing, similar to the one used in Singapore.

(NZ) 'The Warehouse' in New Zealand has a surplus of Easter Eggs they've been unable to sell because they are closed due to Lockdown, so they're donating thousands of Easter Eggs to Women's Refuge and Kiwi Harvest. Kiwi Harvest is a food rescue charity that collects good food before it goes to waste, distributing it to those in need.

(NZ) Easter is coming up and to prevent people from travelling over the 4-day weekend roadblocks will be set up. The Police will man these. Some locals of popular spots have already set up their own blockades telling non-locals to, quite bluntly: FUCK OFF BACK TO WHERE YOU COME FROM!

(NZ) There are 50 new cases in New Zealand today.

(SINGAPORE) Singapore has banned gatherings of any size in homes and public spaces. This means no parties or family gatherings with people not already living together.

(US) Over 17 million people have filed for unemployment

claims in the last three weeks.

(US) Amazon.com have stopped shipping books to certain countries outside the United States. Due to the lack of flights they can't guarantee that 'physical' books and products will arrive. In New Zealand the only way to receive a book from Amazon is by digital download.

APRIL 9 THURSDAY

(GLOBAL) The number of Covid-19 deaths has passed 100,000. (107,047).

(AUS) In Australia, the NRL, (National Rugby League), has announced its intentions to restart the 2020 season competition on May 28. The restarted season will depend on what Government restrictions are in place at that time. Although many people would welcome a return to the competition it hardly seems likely considering the impact that Covid-19 is having on the world.

(NZ) The fifteenth day of Lockdown, Alert Level 4.

(NZ) All travellers returning home from overseas will now be quarantined in one of 18 hotels paid for by the Government.

(NZ) Flight Centre NZ has stood down 300 employees and closed 58 retail shops across the country. When travel restrictions are lifted the employees will be welcomed back with open arms.

(NZ) Bauer Media NZ has closed its doors permanently. They are responsible for New Zealand's biggest newsstand magazines. Thus there will be no more: Woman's Day; NZ Woman's Weekly; The Listener; North and South; and others. These magazines have been in New Zealand for decades; The Woman's Weekly since 1932.

(NZ) It's not the Easter holidays yet but Police are already turning people away from travelling out of town to visit relations or go to their Bach or holiday home.

(NZ) Today there are 29 new cases. 317 people have recovered from 1239 cases. 14 people are in hospital, two in critical condition.

APRIL 10 FRIDAY

(NZ) The sixteenth day of Lockdown, Alert Level 4.

(NZ) New Zealand has had its second death related to Covid-19; a Christchurch lady in her 90's. She was one of 20 residents transferred to Burwood Hospital from Rosewood Rest Home. Rosewood is a 64-bed rest home and hospital. It is divided into three sections: one for rest home residents; one for people requiring hospital care; and one for dementia patients who also need hospital-level care. There are fears there may be more deaths associated with the Rest Home.

(NZ) There are 44 new cases today, bringing the total up to 1283. There have been 373 recoveries.

(NZ) Significant clusters in New Zealand are:

1. Bluff Wedding (87 cases)
2. Marist College (84 cases)
3. Redoubt Bar in Matamata (69 cases)
4. An Auckland Function (34 cases)
5. The World Hereford Conference (33 cases)
6. Rosewood Rest Home (28 cases)
7. An Auckland Business (28 cases)
8. A Wellington Travel Group (to USA) (16 cases)
9. Ruby Princess Cruise Ship* (16 cases)
10. An Auckland Travel Group (to USA)* (15 cases)
11. A Waikato Rest Home (14 cases)
12. A Wellington Wedding (13 cases)

*New since the March 31 list.

(YEMEN) Yemen has its first case of the Coronavirus.

APRIL 11 SATURDAY

(GLOBAL) There are now 1.6 million cases of Covid-19 worldwide. 97,000 people have died.

(NZ) The seventeenth day of Lockdown, Alert Level 4.

(NZ) There are two more deaths in New Zealand today. One is a man in his 70's connected to the same Rest Home (Rosewood) as yesterday's death. The other is a man in his 80's who died in Wellington Hospital. He was associated with the Bluff Wedding cluster. The New Zealand death toll is now 4.

(NZ) New Zealand has 29 new cases today. The total number of New Zealand cases is 1312. Out of this 422 people have recovered.

(SWEDEN) Although they won't admit it, Sweden appears to be using a 'Herd Immunity' strategy to combat the virus. Unlike most other countries they have not applied any Lockdown. The Swedish Government is encouraging 'the right behaviour.' They encourage each individual to take responsibility for their own health and the health of others; recommending that people aged over 70 limit close contact with other people. Sweden has a population of 10 million people, twice that of New Zealand. Currently they have 10,151 cases of Covid-19. Of this total 887 people have died.

(US) The United States has recorded 24,474 deaths. They now have the most Coronavirus deaths of any country in the world.

(US) People are being buried in mass graves in New York State. The State now has more Covid-19 cases than any single country. There are 162,000 cases and 7844 people have died. The United States as a whole has over 467,000 cases.

APRIL 12 SUNDAY

(GLOBAL) There are 1,777,666 cases around the world. 108,867 people have died. 423,744 people have recovered.

(EUROPE) Italy has over 147,000 cases. Spain has 161,857.

(CH) Wet Markets in Wuhan are reopening. Wet Markets are markets traditionally in the open air that sell fresh produce and live animals, such as fish. The Wet Markets in Wuhan are uncertain of their future as customers associate the Covid-19 virus as originating at one of them. In January China ordered a temporary ban on the trade and consumption of wildlife.

(NZ) The eighteenth day of Lockdown, Alert Level 4.

(NZ) Thirteen of the sixteen New Zealanders trapped on the Greg Mortimer Cruise ship off Uruguay have arrived back in New Zealand after weeks of desperate pleas for the New Zealand Government to rescue them.

(NZ) There are 18 new cases today. 49 people have recovered bringing the recovered total to 471.

(UK) Almost 80,000 people have tested positive for Coronavirus in Britain. The death toll is 9875. 12% of their total cases.

(VATICAN CITY) The Pope has given Easter Mass in an almost empty St Peter's Basilica. He called on Political Leaders to work actively for the common good. The whole world is suffering and needs to be united in facing the pandemic. He said that: 'his thoughts were with those directly affected by the virus.'

APRIL 13 MONDAY

(ITALY) Andrea Bocelli has performed an Easter Concert from the empty steps of Milan's largest Church. It was streamed live on YouTube interspersed with footage of empty Italian streets.

(NZ) The nineteenth day of Lockdown, Alert Level 4.

(NZ) Another man associated with the Rosewood Rest Home cluster has died. This is the third death from Rosewood in four days. The death toll in New Zealand now stands at 5.

(NZ) New Zealand has 19 new cases today bringing the total to 1349. Of these 546 people have recovered.

(UK) Boris Johnson has recovered and left hospital. He's given thanks to two nurses in particular. One, Luis, is from Portugal; the other, Jenny McGee is a New Zealander from Invercargill. Boris spent three nights in Intensive Care and it's been said that it could have gone 'either way.'

(UK) Tim Brooke Taylor, the English comedian that was part of 'The Goodies' has died of Covid-19. He joins a long list of International Show Business people who have succumbed to the disease, some being: Adam Schlesinger; Alan Merrill; Allen Davian; Allen Garfield; Andrew Jack; Charles Gregory; Eddie Large; Floyd Cardoz; Hilary Heath; Joe Diffie; John Prine; Ken Shimura; Maria Mercader; Mark Blum; Patricia Bosworth; Terence McNally; and Tom Dempsey.

(US) Anthony Fauci, the Director of the National Institute of Allergy and Infectious Diseases, has said that if they had, right from the beginning, shut everything down, things may have been different. He says that if the President had listened to the medical experts they could've saved more lives. President Trump has responded with: #FireFauci.

APRIL 14 TUESDAY

(AUSTRIA) Austria has allowed thousands of small shops to reopen as they ease up on restrictions. Larger shops, shopping centres, and hairdressers, are due to follow on May 1st.

(NZ) The twentieth day of Lockdown, Alert Level 4.

(NZ) Four people have died of Covid-19 today in New Zealand. This is New Zealand's most fatal day since the pandemic began. Three of the cases are associated with the Rosewood cluster. The death toll stands at 9.

(NZ) There are 17 new cases in New Zealand bringing the total to 1366 cases. 82 people recovered today making a total of 628 people having recovered from the virus. That's almost half.

(NZ) The Easter Weekend Road Toll is zero for the first time since 2012. There were 500 checkpoints set up around New Zealand to prevent people 'holidaying' instead of observing Lockdown restrictions. Over 800 people breached the Lockdown rules over the weekend. 100 people were prosecuted.

(NZ) In New Zealand Burger King has gone into Receivership. Apparently the inability to earn revenue has created significant challenges for the company. They can't pay rent or creditors. Burger King has 83 stores and 2600 staff in New Zealand.

(US) The New York City death toll has passed 10,000. This total includes people who were not tested for Covid-19 but were presumed to have died from it.

APRIL 15 WEDNESDAY

(GLOBAL) There are 2 million confirmed cases worldwide. The total climbed from 1 million to 2 million in less than two weeks. The worldwide death toll has passed 129,000.

(DENMARK) Denmark is reopening Daycare centres and some schools as European countries start loosening their lockdowns.

(NZ) The twenty-first day of Lockdown, Alert Level 4.

(NZ) In New Zealand Prime Minister Jacinda Ardern and other Members of Parliament will take a 20% pay cut for the next 6 months. This is in recognition of those New Zealanders that are reliant on wage subsidies, taking pay cuts, and losing their jobs as a result of Covid-19.

(NZ) There are 20 new cases today. New Zealand's total is 1386. Out of this total 728 people have recovered. Over half of New Zealand's Covid-19 cases have recovered.

(SPAIN) Spain has allowed construction and manufacturing to resume.

(US) President Trump has halted US funding of the World Health Organisation because he says it has 'failed in it's basic duty,' in its response to the Coronavirus Outbreak. Many believe he is trying to deflect criticism away from how he's handled the outbreak in the United States.

(US) In Michigan, protesters have gathered to demand that Governor Gretchen Whitmer ease restrictions and allow them to go back to work. They believe that Whitmer's 'Stay At Home' executive order is excessive and beyond her authority. Whitmer said that the protest, (called 'Operation Gridlock'), endangered lives and might just have made the situation in Michigan worse. Some of the protesters are walking around carrying

rifles.

APRIL 16 THURSDAY

(NZ) The twenty-second day of Lockdown, Alert Level 4.

(NZ) Prime Minister Jacinda Ardern has revealed the guidelines for Alert Level 3, which could come into effect next week if things go to plan.

- We will still be expected to remain in our bubbles but the bubble can be extended a little to include further family members or support people.

- Surfing and fishing restrictions (and some other hobbies) have been lifted as long as it's not treated as a new activity (i.e. don't take up surfing).

- Kids up to Year 10 can return to school if they have to but it's preferred that they still stay at home. Chances are a lot of children will have to go to school as it's said that half a million people will now be able to return to their work.

- Certain businesses will be able to reopen (Construction and businesses that don't have face-to-face interactions). Bars, restaurants and hairdressers and the like must remain closed. Businesses that offer takeaways or have an online shopping option may re-open. Drive-through restaurants like McDonalds and KFC may open their Drive-thru's only.

- Travel is still restricted like it is in Alert Level 4, meaning you should stay in your local area unless you need to travel for work or school reasons.

- Up to ten people can gather for funerals or weddings but there are to be no receptions.

The Government will decide on Monday whether or not they think it's safe to leave the Alert Level 4 Lockdown and go to Alert Level 3.

(NZ) Deputy Prime Minister Winston Peters says New Zealand might open its borders to Australia sooner than the rest of the world, if both countries continued to manage the pandemic. He says: 'It's almost as if we've got a Trans-Tasman bubble between our two countries, and if the figures keep on going that way then that is a serious possibility.' ('Tasman' refers to the Tasman Sea that lies between New Zealand and Australia).

(NZ) There are 15 new cases today bringing the total to 1401. Of that total 770 have recovered.

(US) 5.2 million Americans filed for unemployment claims last week. This brings the total to 22 million people making unemployment claims since President Trump declared a National Emergency four weeks ago.

(US) President Trump says that US States will be able to reopen one step at a time instead of all at once. Governors can begin phased openings at the State-wide or county-by-county level.

APRIL 17 FRIDAY

(NZ) The twenty-third day of Lockdown, Alert Level 4.

(NZ) Two more people have died in New Zealand. One is a lady in her 80's associated with the Rosewood Rest Home cluster. The other is a man in his nineties associated with the Matamata Bar cluster.

(NZ) For the first time in almost a month New Zealand's new cases have fallen to single figures. Today there are 8 new cases bringing our total to 1409. 816 people have recovered.

(NZ) Taranaki has not had a new case of Covid-19 in the last 16 days. There are still some people sick or isolating but there have been no new cases for over two weeks. New Zealand might implement a regional restrictions rule where those areas with no new cases for some time can ease up on their restrictions if they stay within their "Regional Bubble." This will mean manning the borders, but the Police did that over Easter so it shouldn't be a problem. Auckland and Canterbury are still seeing new daily cases.

(UK) In England Captain Tom Moore, a Second World War veteran, has walked 100 laps of his garden before his 100th birthday. He's 99 and was hoping to raise £1000. So far he's raised £20 million!! All of the money is going to the NHS. Captain Moore says that as long as the money keeps coming in he'll keep walking.

(US) Texas Governor, Greg Abbot, has made Executive Orders to begin the process of reopening the State of Texas, beginning in May. Texas will be one of the first States to loosen restrictions.

APRIL 18 SATURDAY

(FAROES) What's happened in the Faroe Islands has been considered a success. The Faroe Islands are an isolated territory of Denmark with a significant salmon farming industry. Because of their salmon industry they have a very sophisticated laboratory, installed after a major salmon disease hit the industry about twenty years ago. A Veterinarian called Debes Christiansen adapted his salmon-testing lab to test for Covid-19 in humans. By February 2020 up to 600 people were able to be tested per day. 10% of the population has been tested and out of the 61,000 people on the Faroes only 184 have tested

positive. There have been no new cases since the 5th of April. 173 people have recovered leaving only 11 still in isolation. No one is critical and there have been no deaths.

(NZ) The twenty-fourth day of Lockdown, Alert Level 4.

(NZ) There have been 13 new cases reported today in New Zealand putting the country back up into double figures after yesterday's 8. The total is now 1422 cases with 867 people recovered. The number of deaths have gone up to 12 (from 11) as, via post mortem, a man who died earlier in the week has been confirmed as a victim of Covid-19.

APRIL 19 SUNDAY

(CHILE) Chile's Government is planning to issue 'Immunity Certificates' to people who have recovered from the virus and completed a period of isolation.

(CH) China's reported scale of the outbreak in their country has been challenged by the United States, the UK, France and some other countries. Even in China there has been speculation that the officially reported number is wrong. China has admitted that 1290 more people died in Wuhan than was originally reported. This is 50% more than the original total of 2579 on Friday. The nationwide number for China is now 3869.

(ISRAEL) Israel has passed some new regulations that significantly relax their Lockdown. Stores that operate in a small space, (not shopping centers), can open but only two customers are allowed inside at a time. Sports are allowed in pairs, 500 metres from home. People must wear masks in public places or they will face a possible fine. Up to 10 people may attend weddings but they must stay 2 metres apart.

(NZ) The twenty-fifth day of Lockdown, Alert Level 4.

(NZ) New Zealand has 9 new cases today; back under double figures after yesterday's little blip. The total is now 1431 with 912 recovered. Three boys under the age of one (in Southland and Waikato) have contracted the virus.

(UK) Coronavirus has infected 2000 United Kingdom Rest Homes but the deaths are not included in the daily tally. This has led to accusations that the UK is not giving the correct number of deaths. It's thought that maybe 40% of Covid-19 deaths might actually be in Rest Homes.

APRIL 20 MONDAY

(NZ) The twenty-sixth day of Lockdown, Alert Level 4.

(NZ) Prime Minister Jacinda Ardern announced today that Alert Level 4 will be extended for another week, then New Zealand will drop to Alert Level 3 at 11:59PM next Monday. The country will then remain at Alert Level 3 for at least two weeks. The decision whether to move to Level 2 is set to be made on the 11th of May.

(NZ) New Zealand has a transmission rate of 0.48, which means that someone with the virus will pass it on to 0.48 other people on average. This is an incredible result considering that one person has the potential to infect hundreds.

(NZ) There are 9 new cases in NZ bringing the total to 1440. Of this 974 people have recovered.

(US) President Trump has said that he intends to temporarily close the United States to people trying to immigrate into the country to live and work. This is being done to protect American workers from foreign competition.

APRIL 21 TUESDAY

(GLOBAL) The virus has done more damage to the Oil Industry than the Electric Car. The price of a barrel of Oil has plummeted to $-3.70 a barrel. Because less people are using oil there's nowhere to store new production. It's not sure if we'll see a price reduction at the pumps though.

(CAN) In Canada a man has gone on a shooting rampage killing 18 people. He was wearing a Police Uniform and driving a 'look-alike' Police Vehicle. The gunman was shot and killed.

(NZ) The twenty-seventh day of Lockdown, Alert Level 4.

(NZ) Prime Minister Jacinda Ardern has said that getting out of Alert Level 3 will depend on how well New Zealanders follow the rules. 'It's within everyone's power and this is why it is a collective effort and why we're a team of five million.' New Zealand is currently at Alert Level 4 but will be moving to Alert Level 3 next Monday, at 11:59PM.

(NZ) A New Zealander in his forties has died of Covid-19 in Peru. He missed the repatriation flight organised by the New Zealand Government. His family filed a missing person report and Interpol got involved. The man was found dead in his flat. His death is not included in the number of New Zealand deaths because it's been added to Peru's tally.

(NZ) New Zealand had another death today bringing the total to 13. The woman, in her 70's, is part of an Auckland cluster associated with St Margaret's Rest Home and Hospital. 25 cases have been linked to the rest home.

(NZ) There are 5 new cases today; the lowest number in over a month. The total number of cases is 1445. Over a thousand people have recovered.

(NETHERLANDS) The Netherlands have extended their ban

on major public events to September the 1st. This includes music festivals and professional sports. Because of the slowing of Covid-19 Daycares and elementary schools could possibly open in May.

APRIL 22 WEDNESDAY

(NZ) The twenty-eighth day of Lockdown, Alert Level 4.

(NZ) There are 6 new cases in New Zealand today. The total is now 1451. The country's total recoveries are 1036. There was another death though, bringing the total to 14. She was a lady in her 80's associated with the Rosewood Rest Home cluster.

(NZ) Here are the significant clusters in New Zealand as of today

1. Bluff Wedding (98 cases)
2. Marist College (93 cases)
3. Redoubt Matamata Bar (76 cases)
4. Rosewood Rest Home (50 cases)
5. World Hereford Conference (40 cases)
6. An Auckland Function (39 cases)
7. An Auckland Business (30 cases)
8. St Margaret's Rest Home* (28 cases)
9. Ruby Princess Cruise Ship (22 cases)
10. A Christchurch Rest Home* (20 cases)
11. A Wellington Travel Group (to USA) (16 cases)
12. An Auckland Travel Group (to USA) (16 cases)
13. A Wellington Wedding (13 cases)
14. A Christchurch Workplace* (10 cases)

*New since April 10

(UK) Human trials for a Covid-19 vaccine are to start in the UK on Thursday. The UK has apparently invested more money in finding a vaccine than any other country. It's believed that the best way to defeat Coronavirus will be with a vaccine.

(US) At the Bronx Zoo in New York City four more tigers and

JASON KOMENE

three lions have tested positive for Covid-19.

APRIL 23 THURSDAY

(AUS) Australian Prime Minister Scott Morrison has revealed that New Zealand is likely to be the first country that Australia will reopen its border to as it looks to relax Covid-19 restrictions.

(NZ) The twenty-ninth day of Lockdown, Alert Level 4.

(NZ) Two people in New Zealand died today. This brings the total of New Zealand deaths related to Covid-19 to 16. One was a Dunedin woman in her sixties. The other was a man associated with the Rosewood Rest Home cluster. 9 of the 16 New Zealand deaths have been related to Rosewood.

(NZ) Three new cases today.

(SINGAPORE) Singapore had been hailed as an example of a country that had handled Covid-19 really well. Now it's not so good. There has been a recent spike in cases. Singapore had been fine against incoming infections by instituting quarantines and contact tracing. They also didn't allow 'positive' people back into the community, keeping them in hospital rather than home quarantine. Unfortunately there were clusters building that were not discovered, or tested until too late. Some of these were amongst Singapore's vast migrant worker population, many of who live in cramped dormitories where the virus 'was a time bomb waiting to explode.'

Here are some Singapore figures. About two weeks ago (April 7) they had about the same number of cases as New Zealand currently has, (1481). Now they have 11,178 (as of April 21). This is almost an increase of 10,000 in two weeks.

(UK) Human trials of a Covid-19 vaccine have begun in the UK. Their vaccine uses a small section of the Covid-19 code packaged into a harmless virus. It's hoped that delivering this

into the body will teach the immune system how to fight off
the real disease.

APRIL 24 FRIDAY

(GLOBAL) The Ruby Princess Cruise-Ship has had more Covid-19 cases and deaths than any other Cruise-ship, even more than the Diamond Princess.

Ruby Princess (852 Cases 24 Deaths)
Diamond Princess (712 Cases 14 Deaths)
Grand Princess (122 Cases 7 Deaths)
Artania (89 Cases 4 Deaths)
Zaandam (11 Cases 4 Deaths)
Costa Luminosa (36 Cases 3 Deaths)
Oasis of the Seas (14 Cases 3 Deaths)
Coral Princess (12 Cases 3 Deaths)
Costa Fascinosa (43 Cases 3 Deaths)
Voyager of the Seas (39 Cases 2 Deaths)
Celebrity Eclipse (10 Cases 2 Deaths)
Silver Shadow (2 Cases 1 Death)
Norwegian Breakaway (3 Cases 1 Death)
Celebrity Solstice (20 Cases 1 Death)
Ovation of the Sea (79 Cases 1 Death)
Costa Favolosa (13 Cases 1 Death)
Greg Mortimer (128 Cases 1 Death)
Symphony of the Seas (31 Cases 1 Death)

(INDONESIA) Starting this week Indonesia will temporarily ban Domestic and International air and sea travel. The ban will apply until May 31. Cargo transport is exempted, as are repatriation flights.

(NZ) The thirtieth day of Lockdown, Alert Level 4.

(NZ) New Zealand has another death. A man in his 60's associated with the Rosewood cluster. It's the 10th death associated with Rosewood. The country has 5 new cases bringing the total to 1456 cases. 1095 of these have recovered. 17 have died.

(NZ) Petrol is down to $1.86/litre. Usually it sits well over $2. The lower worldwide demand and sales for petrol and oil has made for the drop in price.

(US) The death toll in the United States has passed 50,000 people.

APRIL 25 SATURDAY

(NZ) The thirty-first day of Lockdown, Alert Level 4.

(NZ) Today is ANZAC day; a day where New Zealanders and Australians remember those who served and fell in past wars. Because of the Lockdown this year there are no official parades or ceremonies like there usually would be. This morning, up and down the country, New Zealanders rose before sunrise and stood at their letterboxes as part of a 'Stand At Dawn' campaign.

(NZ) Another death brings the tally to 18 people having died of Covid-19 in New Zealand. There are 5 new cases today.

(US) President Trump has been criticised for suggesting that it might be possible to treat Covid-19 by injecting people with disinfectant. Experts have had to jump in and strongly warn people against following the President's suggestion. The makers of Lysol are imploring the public not to put their product in their bodies.

APRIL 26 SUNDAY

(GLOBAL) 203,331 people in the world have died of Covid-19.

(GLOBAL) 889,049 people have recovered from the virus.

(WHO) The World Health Organisation has said that there is no evidence that those that have recovered can not be reinfected. They are concerned that some Governments are thinking of implementing an 'Immunity Passport' that enables recovered people to pretty much go anywhere they like.

(ITALY) Italy's Manufacturing Industry will start reopening on May 4. Schools are to remain closed until September.

(NZ) The thirty-second day of Lockdown, Alert Level 4.

(NZ) New Zealand has 9 new cases today. The total is now 1470. The number of people recovered is 1142. That's 78% recovered.

(UK) Captain Tom Moore, the 99 year-old World War Two veteran who raised millions of pounds walking around his garden, has gone to #1 on the UK music charts with a cover version of "You'll Never Walk Alone." It's a duet with Michael Ball. Tom Moore is the oldest person to reach #1 and will still be #1 when he turns a hundred on Thursday.

APRIL 27 MONDAY

(GLOBAL) There are now 3 million cases of Covid-19 in the world. 12 days after reaching 2 million, and 25 days after reaching 1 million. The United States alone has passed 1 million cases, recording a third of all cases so far. Since the beginning of April the United States have been reporting over 20,000 cases per day.

(NZ) The thirty-third day of Lockdown, Alert Level 4.

(NZ) One lady died today in New Zealand. She was part of the St Margaret's cluster. This brings the death toll to 19. New Zealand has 5 new cases today while 6 previous cases have been rescinded. The total number of cases is now 1469, one less than yesterday.

(NZ) Tonight, at 11:59 PM New Zealand leaves the Alert Level 4 Lockdown and enters Alert Level 3.

APRIL 28 TUESDAY

(C-19) According to the American Association for Cancer Research, cancer patients who develop Covid-19 have nearly three times as much chance of dying than the general public.

(NZ) Today is the first day of Alert Level 3. It's been thirty-four days since Lockdown began.

(NZ) Under Alert Level 3 there are a few changes but pretty much it will remain the same as Alert Level 4. Some of the changes are:

- Schools will be open to students up to Year 10
- Takeaways can open as long as deliveries are contactless, or just pick up orders. Restaurants with drive-thru's can only give the drive-thru option.
- Shopping must be contactless click and collect in addition to online orders.
- Sports and Recreation. Team sports are still out but you can go swimming, surfing, fishing, and do other low-risk non-motorised activities.
- The Workforce is expected to double. Plumbers, electricians and builders can start again as long as they keep their distance.
- Travel restrictions are pretty much the same as Alert Level 4 except if you need to get to work, or a school, or travel for medical reasons.

(NZ) Practically every McDonalds, KFC and Burger King has had long drive-thru queues all day. Some people are waiting up to three hours for their order.

(NZ) New Zealand has three new cases today. The total is 1472 with 19 deaths.

(NZ) Under Alert Level 3 those people who were unable to

get home before Level 4 Lockdown restrictions were enforced are now allowed to return to their homes.

APRIL 29 WEDNESDAY

(GLOBAL) Over 1 million people have recovered from the virus, (1,014,776).

(C-19) Two independent studies have been published, (by the New England Journal of Medicine, and the Lancet), related to the stability of the Covid-19 virus on various surfaces:

Copper - Up to 4 hours

Cardboard - Up to a day

Wood - Up to 2 days

Glass - Up to 4 days

Paper - Up to 4 days

Stainless Steel - 3 to 7 days

Plastic - 3 to 7 days

(NZ) Today is the second day of Alert Level 3. It's been thirty-five days since Lockdown began.

(NZ) Deputy Prime Minister Winston Peters has revealed in a speech that at the beginning of the pandemic New Zealand Health Officials pushed strongly to completely shut New Zealand's borders to everyone. This would have meant stranding thousands of New Zealanders in foreign countries. Cabinet ministers rejected the idea, refusing to forsake New Zealanders stuck overseas. 80,000 New Zealanders have returned home since the 14th of March. 45,000 foreign nationals departed New Zealand during the Level 4 Lockdown.

(NZ) A large crowd gathered today outside a Burger Fuel in Auckland. They were obviously not adhering to the Social Distancing protocol as they waited for their orders. The Government has said that if businesses can't, or won't, deal with the Social Distancing rules then they'll have to close down. The crowds took Burger Fuel by surprise and they have said that they are already working on better systems of crowd control.

(NZ) Today there are 2 new cases bringing the total to 1474. Of that 1229 people have recovered.

APRIL 30 THURSDAY

(NZ) Today is the third day of Alert Level 3. It's been thirty-six days since Lockdown began.

(NZ) School started yesterday and 2% of all students actually went. The rest are supposed to be doing their schooling via computer at home. Out of a school roll of 800 students 12 went to Francis Douglas Memorial College in New Plymouth. Mana College in Porirua, just north of Wellington, had one student turn up.

(NZ) New Zealand has three further cases today bringing the total to 1476. The number of people who have recovered is 1241.

(COMOROS) Comoros has its first case of the Coronavirus.

(TAJIKISTAN) Tajikistan has its first case of the Coronavirus.

(GLOBAL) 219 countries and territories have had cases of the Coronavirus. The majority of countries and territories reported their first cases in March, (139 countries). In April ten countries and territories reported first cases: Caribbean Netherlands; Comoros; Falkland Islands; Malawi; Saint Pierre Miquelon; Sao Tome and Principe; South Sudan; Tajikistan; Western Sahara; and Yemen.

(GLOBAL) The following 138 countries and territories reported their first cases in March: Albania; Andorra; Angola; Anguilla; Antigua and Barbuda; Argentina; Armenia; Aruba; Bahamas; Bangladesh; Barbados; Belize; Benin; Bermuda; Bhutan; Bolivia; Bosnia and Herzegovina; Botswana; British Virgin Islands; Brunei; Bulgaria; Burkina Faso; Burundi; Cabo Verde; Cameroon; Cayman Islands; Central African Republic; Chad; Channel Islands; Chile; Colombia; Congo; Costa Rica; Cuba;

Curaçao; Cyprus; Czech Republic; DR Congo; Djibouti; Dominican Republic; El Salvador; Equatorial Guinea; Eritrea; Eswatini; Ethiopia; Faroe Islands; Fiji; French Guinea; French Polynesia; Gabon; Gambia; Ghana; Gibraltar; Greenland; Grenada; Guadalupe; Guam; Guatemala; Guinea; Guinea-Bissau; Guyana; Haiti; Honduras; Hungary; Indonesia; Isle Of Man; Ivory Coast; Jamaica; Jordan; Kazakhstan; Kenya; Kyrgyzstan; Laos; Latvia; Liberia; Libya; Liechtenstein; Madagascar; Maldives; Mali; Malta; Martinique; Mauritania; Mauritius; Mayotte; Moldova; Mongolia; Montenegro; Montserrat; Morocco; Mozambique; Myanmar; Namibia; New Caledonia; Nicaragua; Niger; Palestine; Panama; Papua New Guinea; Paraguay; Peru; Poland; Portugal; Réunion; Rwanda; Saudi Arabia; St Barth; Saint Kitts and Nevis; Saint Lucia; Saint Martin; St Vincent and the Grenadines; Senegal; Serbia; Seychelles; Sierra Leone; Sint Maaten; Slovakia; Slovenia; Somalia; South Africa; Sudan; Suriname; Syria; Tanzania; Timor-Leste; Togo; Trinidad and Tobago; Tunisia; Turkey; Turks and Caicos Islands; Uganda; Ukraine; Uruguay; Uzbekistan; Vatican City; Venezuela; Zambia; and Zimbabwe.

(GLOBAL) The following 35 countries and territories reported their first cases in February: Algeria; Austria; Azerbaijan; Bahrain; Belarus; Belgium; Croatia; Denmark; Egypt; Ecuador; Estonia; Georgia; Greece; Iceland; Iran; Iraq; Ireland; Israel, Kuwait; Lebanon; Lithuania; Luxembourg; Mexico; Monaco; the Netherlands; New Zealand; Nigeria; North Macedonia; Norway; Oman; Pakistan; Qatar; Romania; San Marino; and Switzerland.

(GLOBAL) The following 27 countries and territories reported their first cases in January, (or earlier in the case of China): Australia; Cambodia; Canada; China; Finland; France; Germany; Hong Kong; India; Italy; Japan; Macau; Malaysia; Nepal; Philippines; Russia; Singapore; Spain; Sweden; South Korea; Sri Lanka; Taiwan; Thailand; the United Arab Emirates; the United Kingdom; the United States of America; and Vietnam.

(GLOBAL) There are still Countries and territories that have not had (or reported) any cases of Coronavirus. Most of the following are isolated island nations in the Pacific Ocean: American Samoa; Ascension; Christmas Island; Cocos Islands, Cook Islands; Federated States of Micronesia; Kiribati; Lesotho; Marshall Islands; Nauru; Niue; Norfolk Island; North Korea; Palau; Pitcairn Islands; Saint Helena; Sahrawi Arab Democratic Republic; Samoa; Solomon Islands; South Ossetia; Svalbard; Tokelau; Tonga; Tristan da Cunha; Turkmenistan; Tuvalu; Vanuatu; and, Wallis and Futuna.

(ANTARCTICA) Antarctica is the only Continent in the world with no cases of Covid-19.

APRIL: SURREAL

It was surreal.

We were facing possibly the greatest calamity ever to hit New Zealand, yet we still had power and food and water. We had heating and television. We had our homes. We were with our loved ones. We had access to essential services if we required them and could buy groceries if we needed them. Nothing was broken. Nothing was destroyed. It was like we'd been hit by the softest disaster ever. We were 'going early and going hard' in the safety of our armchairs while watching Netflix.

It was surreal.

You could point at any random person on television and say: "That person's in Lockdown. Right now, somewhere in the world, that person right there on the screen, is self-isolating." Tom Cruise, Paul McCartney, Stephen Spielberg, the lady who does the voice for Bart Simpson, each of the names in the credits at the end of every show, every single one of them, was in lockdown! Never before had anyone been able to know what everyone else in the world was doing at the same time.

It was surreal.

Actually, not everyone on television was in Lockdown. Not Jacinda and Ashley. New Zealand's most watched television show during Lockdown had not even existed a month earlier. Almost every day millions tuned in at 1PM to hear the latest from our Prime Minister and Director General of Health. We were filled in on the latest new cases, the number of recoveries, and whether or not the virus had killed another person. We'd also be updated on the latest developments concerning New Zealand and the world of Covid-19. After each session Jacinda and Ashley would throw themselves open to questions from the gathered Press, who were just waiting to pick apart everything that had been said.

It was surreal.

I tried to explain to my 13 year-old son that what was happening in the world was something that no living person had ever been through before. No one could even have imagined it. The entire shutting-down of the world was unprecedented.

It was surreal.

My hometown had become a ghost town, the streets were empty; footpaths were devoid of pedestrians. The skatepark by the old primary school... deserted! (That place was never empty, all the local kids hung out there, but now they were nowhere to be seen). The road to New Plymouth... nothing! It was a pleasure to drive along empty roads and not have to deal with cars and trucks and tractors and some tailgater trying to push you to go faster. Rural roads are usually riddled with possums and rabbits, victims of traffic, but the traffic was gone, and so too was the roadkill.

It was surreal.

We practiced social distancing and kept two meters away from strangers. We also kept two meters away from acquaintances and people we'd known all our lives. Even though we knew it was unlikely that the other person was infected it was mutually agreed that we respect their social bubble and maintain the required distance of separation. If people kept their distance then you didn't get too upset with the fact that they were presuming that you were infected.

It was surreal.

Last year we would have either scoffed at someone wearing a mask, or we would have found it in some way offensive, (after all, New Zealand is a clean, green country so why the mask, oh, I get it, you think I'm carrying something contagious. Well screw you!) Now, thanks to Covid-19, those sentiments are gone. In fact now we were the one's that were wearing the masks. Even before Lockdown pharmacies were selling out of the things. The time for ridicule or offence was gone as every house was building a stockpile. Mask wearing wasn't mandatory but it was certainly not uncommon to suddenly see people of all ages sporting one.

It was surreal.

We were forced to spend a lot of time with the people we live with. Unless your job was considered essential we were stuck with our bubble-people for weeks. There were not a lot of places where we could escape. The endless days of Lockdown tested even the strongest relationships, and being together drove some people apart.

It was surreal.

A lot of kids wished they could go back to school. Lockdown wasn't anything like the school holidays because you were trapped at home and being trapped at home was hardly fun. You couldn't go to the movies, or the shops, or the skatepark, and you couldn't visit your friends of have them over. And what's worse, the schools still expected you to do homework!

It was surreal.

Some people who were hardly ever without their phones, suddenly craved more than just contact-via-texting. They missed actual physical contact with people that weren't part of their bubble. Some would breach Lockdown restrictions and risk prosecution to meet up with people they needed to see, of course taking their phones with them.

It was surreal.

There were people who didn't agree with the Lockdown restrictions. The idea that the Government could order people what to do didn't hold well with some, and they disobeyed the rules in a variety of ways; often to the harsh disapproval of those adhering to the Lockdown restrictions and not afraid to vent their anger. Many Lockdown breaches were seen and reported to the police. Some offenders recanted their ways. Some were fined for repeated offences. Some were jailed.

It was surreal.

The crime rate went down. You would have to be a very

brazen, (or stupid), burglar to expect to break into any house and not be met by the occupants doing their Lockdown thing. To add further to the burglar's woes, anyone new and acting suspiciously in the neighbourhood was likely to be noticed and reported, by vigilant house occupants hoping to dob in someone breaching Lockdown restrictions.

It was surreal.

Some people discovered that they didn't actually need a fancy office in a big city building to do their work, and that they could be just as productive working from home. Even with the kids making a ruckus in the room next door.

It was surreal.

Some people found that they were 'essential' for the continuation of New Zealand, while others found themselves jobless. Careers that were thought to be safe were suddenly gone, and people used to being in the higher-tax bracket were suddenly applying for positions in Supermarkets.

It was surreal.

Despite assurances that Supermarkets and Pharmacies would be remaining open there was panic-buying. Toilet paper didn't run out. Flour, sugar, and yeast did.

It was surreal.

And despite all that was happening around us we were urged by our Prime Minister to be kind and nice to each other, especially those who had been infected by the disease.

It was so real.

Jason Komene 4 May, 2020

MAY 2020

MAY 1 FRIDAY

(AUS) In Australia the NRL (National Rugby League) 2020 competition has been given the go ahead by state officials in New South Wales, Victoria, and Queensland, to start again on May 28. The conditions are that strict social distancing protocols are followed and that the players are regularly tested for Covid-19.

(NZ) Today is the fourth day of Alert Level 3. It's been thirty-seven days since Lockdown began.

(NZ) New Zealand has 3 new cases. The total is now 1479. Of this 1252 people have recovered. There are 6 people in hospital but none are in intensive care.

(N KOREA) There have been concerns over the last three weeks about the health of North Korean leader Kim Jong-un. Nobody has seen him and the rumours have ranged from him being sick to him having died. He resurfaced today very much alive.

MAY 2 SATURDAY

(NZ) Today is the fifth day of Alert Level 3. It's been thirty-eight days since Lockdown began.

(NZ) There is another New Zealand death today and once again it's associated with the Rosewood cluster. New Zealand now has 20 deaths from Covid-19. There are six new cases bringing the total to 1485. Of this total 1263 people have recovered.

(NZ) The NZ Government has set up an 'International Air Freight Capacity' scheme to maintain trade links with key global markets, thus insuring essential imports such as medical supplies, and exports for companies who have had to charter expensive flights. The first six companies involved are: Air New Zealand, Emirates, Qantas, China Airlines, Freightways Express and Tasman Cargo. This covers a few countries but not everywhere. It's hoped that some of these flights might be able to repatriate stranded New Zealanders.

(RUSSIA) The Mayor of Moscow has said that 2% of the population of Moscow has tested positive for Covid-19. Moscow has a population of about 12.7 million people. 2% would mean that 250,000 people have been infected.

MAY 3 SUNDAY

(NZ) Today is the sixth day of Alert Level 3. It's been thirty-nine days since Lockdown began.

(NZ) Police in New Zealand have received 1200 reports of people breaching Alert Level 3 restrictions. They have prosecuted 135 people and warned 342. Footage on television shows beaches packed with people. Police have had to close down hundreds of parties since Alert Level 3 came into force. They have said that illegal public gatherings would waste all the sacrifices New Zealanders have made to beat Covid-19.

(NZ) The New Zealand Warriors (the New Zealand Rugby League team that plays in the Australian NRL competition) have over the past few weeks been trying to figure out a way to be involved in this year's competition, (considering the strict border controls between Australia and New Zealand). Today it has been announced that they will be permitted to enter Australia but will have to remain there for an indefinite time. They will be required to go into quarantine for 14 days. Talk of a Trans-Tasman 'bubble' means that there might be a chance for the Warriors to be able to return to New Zealand for home matches later in the season.

(NZ) Today New Zealand has 2 new cases. New Zealand has been in single figures since the 17th of April (allowing for one blip on the 18th). It's been discovered by other countries that it can take a long time to achieve zero cases. New Zealand could sit at single figures for a few more weeks before hitting zero; and maintaining zero could be very difficult.

(NZ) New Zealand has had 1487 cases. Of that 1266 have recovered.

MAY 4 MONDAY

(NZ) Today is the seventh day of Alert Level 3. It's been forty days since Lockdown began.

(NZ) New Zealand has zero cases today! For the first time in 49 days New Zealand has recorded no new cases of Covid-19.

MAY 5 TUESDAY

(NZ) Today is the eighth day of Alert Level 3. It's been forty-one days since Lockdown began.

(NZ) New Zealand has had another day of zero cases. The total number of cases has actually gone down one as a previous case has been rescinded. We are now sitting at 1486 cases. 1302 people have recovered.

(NZ) Simon Bridges, the leader of the opposition party, (the National Party), has come up with some policies that National would bring into place if they were voted in at the next election in September. The ideas have been met with some approval from various experts as they are focussed on bringing the economy back into line, something that everyone wants to happen.

MAY 6 WEDNESDAY

(NZ) Today is the ninth day of Alert Level 3. It's been forty-two days since Lockdown began.

(NZ) New Zealand's zero streak has been marred by two new cases. One related to Marist College is confirmed, while the other is a probable case. New Zealand has suffered one more death; a lady from the Rosewood cluster. The death total for New Zealand is now 21. The total number of Covid cases is 1488. 88% of the cases have recovered, (1316).

(SOUTH OSSETIA) South Ossetia, a disputed territory in the South Caucasus, recognised by Russia and literally only a handful of other countries, (regarded by most others as part of Georgia), has confirmed its first three cases.

(UK) The United Kingdom has surpassed Italy as the European country with the most Covid-19 deaths. Italy has 29,315; the UK has 29,427. Both of these numbers relate to people who have been tested and have died. There are probably a lot more who have died but were never tested.

(US) The United States has more deaths than the UK and Italy combined. They have the highest number of cases and deaths in the world. 74,134 people have died in the United States.

MAY 7 THURSDAY

(NZ) Today is the tenth day of Alert Level 3. It's been forty-three days since Lockdown began.

(NZ) New Zealand has one new case. The total is now 1489. Of this total 1332 people have recovered.

(UK) An artwork by UK Street artist, Banksy, has appeared at Southampton Hospital. It shows a young boy kneeling by a wastepaper basket. Spiderman and Batman action figures have been put in the basket, replaced by a new super hero – an NHS nurse. She is wearing a facemask, a nurse's cape and an apron with the Red Cross emblem on it. She's flying like Superman.

MAY 8 FRIDAY

(GLOBAL) The total number of Covid-19 cases has passed the 4 million mark. It has been less than two weeks since the global total was 3 million.

April 2 (1 million cases)

April 15 (2 million cases)

April 27 (3 million cases)

May 8 (4 million cases)

(NZ) Today is the eleventh day of Alert Level 3. It's been forty-four days since Lockdown began.

(NZ) Prime Minister Jacinda Ardern has unveiled what we will see if New Zealand goes to Alert Level 2. She has described it as a 'safer version of normal,' designed to get as many people back to work as possible. We'll be able to go shopping, eat out, get married, travel within New Zealand, go to school, play sport, and see friends – but with strict rules.

- People in bars, restaurants etc. must be seated and separated. Venues that don't do this will be closed down.

- You can see friends, but no parties!

- Hairdressers and beauticians can open but must use protective gear.

- Gyms can open but must have physical distancing in place.

- Tramping, biking, and hunting will be allowed on Conservation land. Motorised boating will also be allowed.

- The New Zealand border will still remain closed to all but New Zealanders returning home.

- New Zealanders will still be encouraged to maintain physical distancing from strangers, but we can be closer to non-strangers, as these people can be contact-traced more easily.

- Gatherings for things like weddings and funerals are allowed but must be no higher than 100 people; even if they are outside.

- The decision to move to Alert Level 2 will be decided on Monday based on the most up-to-date data.

(NZ) New Zealand has one more case taking the total to 1490.

MAY 9 SATURDAY

(NZ) Today is the twelfth day of Alert Level 3. It's been forty-five days since Lockdown began.

(NZ) Yesterday the New Zealand Government released more than 300 documents related to its response to the Covid-19 pandemic. These documents date from January through to April 17. Because of the lateness of the release there have been complaints that the media weren't given enough time to look through the documents and prepare questions.

(NZ) New Zealand has 2 new cases. The total is 1492 with 1368 recoveries.

(S KOREA) South Korea has had an epidemic control program considered to be one of the best in the world, (along with Taiwan, Vietnam, and Singapore). They have done rapid and extensive tests without having to quarantine entire cities. In April they started lifting restrictions. Just days after re-opening the bars in Seoul they have had to shut them all down again due to a single man sparking a new outbreak. More than 1500 people are believed to have visited the three bars the man went to.

(US) Three children have died in New York of a mysterious toxic-shock inflammation syndrome that has links to Covid-19. More than 73 children in New York have been sickened by the rare illness that is similar to Kawasaki's Disease.

MAY 10 SUNDAY

(NZ) Today is the thirteenth day of Alert Level 3. It's been forty-six days since Lockdown began.

(NZ) The documents released late on Friday afternoon, concerning New Zealand's response to the Covid-19 pandemic, show that the New Zealand Government didn't take or consider certain options. Because these options were not revealed to the New Zealand public at the time, there have been some accusations that the Government's policy of 'transparency' has not been adhered to.

(NZ) After the release of the Government Response documents last Friday, an email was sent out telling Labour Ministers to 'dismiss questions' about the Covid-19 response. This has not helped the 'transparency' issue. The sending of the email has been described as a 'clumsy instruction,' that could have been worded better.

(NZ) There are two new cases in New Zealand today. The total is now 1494. Two people remain in hospital and 1371 people have recovered.

(S KOREA) There are fears of a second wave of Covid-19 in South Korea. Officials are trying to contact 1940 people who visited the three nightclubs an asymptomatic 29 year-old Korean went to. South Korea had not had any cases for days. Now they've shot up to 34.

MAY 11 MONDAY

(NZ) Today is the fourteenth day of Alert Level 3. It's been forty-seven days since Lockdown began.

(NZ) Prime Minister Jacinda Ardern has made the announcement that New Zealand will move to Alert Level 2 at 11:59PM on Wednesday. Much of the economy will be open (malls, cinemas, hairdressers etc.). We'll be able to socialise as long as the group contains no more than 10 people. On Friday the number of people allowed to attend a Wedding or a Funeral was 100. This has been dropped back to no more than 10. Schools will reopen next Monday but Bars will have to remain closed for another week. They will be allowed to open on Thursday May 21.

(NZ) China has berated New Zealand for its support of Taiwan's participation at the World Health Organisation as an observer. China wants New Zealand to strictly abide by the 'One China principle' and immediately stop making wrong statements about Taiwan; to avoid damaging 'our bilateral relationship.' The 'One China principle' is a policy asserting that there is only one sovereign state under the name 'China.' It does not recognise Taiwan as an Independent State. Taiwan has reported only 440 Coronavirus cases and seven deaths thanks to early and effective disease prevention controls.

(NZ) New Zealand has three new Covid-19 cases today bringing the total to 1497. There are no new deaths and for the first time since the 22nd of March the number of active cases is under 100. There are 90 people still to recover.

MAY 12 TUESDAY

(GERMANY) There is mounting concern over the potential for a second wave of Covid-19 cases in Germany. Infections have increased dramatically after Germany's first tentative steps to ease its relatively successful Lockdown. This has caused Global concern casting a shadow over the reopening of businesses ranging from hair salons in Paris, to Shanghai Disneyland in China.

(IRELAND) In the past week the Garda (Irish Police Force) have had to use Spit hoods 19 times, (Spit hoods are wire and mesh face coverings, secured over a prisoner's head). Gardai have been deliberately spat or coughed on 64 times since the start of April.

(NZ) Today is the fifteenth day of Alert Level 3. It's been forty-eight days since Lockdown began.

(NZ) New Zealand has no new cases today, the total remaining at 1497. This is the third time in ten days that New Zealand has had zero cases. Two people are still in hospital, neither of them in Intensive Care.

(RUSSIA) Russia has overtaken Italy and Britain, reporting the world's highest tally of cases outside of the United States and Spain. They have 232,243 cases.

(US) President Trump is pushing for the rapid reopening of US states, against the recommendations of health experts.

MAY 13 WEDNESDAY

(BRAZIL) Covid-19 is accelerating in Brazil. They have 177,589 cases, surpassing Germany's 170,508 and almost reaching France's tally of 178,225. Brazil has recorded its deadliest day (881 deaths). Their President has fought Brazilian States over his wish to reopen gyms and beauty parlours, claiming them as 'essential' services. He has said that the economic damage from closing businesses is worse than the disease.

(NZ) Today is the sixteenth day of Alert Level 3. It's been forty-nine days since Lockdown began.

(NZ) The New Zealand Government has passed a new law for Alert Level 2 that allows the Police to enter any premises without a warrant. Originally the law was going to be set for 2 years, but because of opposition it has been changed to 3 months. The reasoning for Warrantless entry is to enforce restrictions on gatherings. Groups of more than 10 are not allowed.

(NZ) The New Zealand Government has listened to the public and adjusted the number of people allowed at funerals and Tangihanga (traditional Maori funeral rites) from 10 up to 50; as long as strict public health measures are in place.

(NZ) Today is the second day in a row with no new cases in New Zealand. At 11:59PM we will be leaving Alert Level 3 and going to Alert Level 2.

(LESOTHO) Lesotho has its first case of the Coronavirus. Lesotho is the last African nation to report its first case of the virus.

MAY 14 THURSDAY

(NZ) New Zealand is now in Alert Level 2. It has been fifty days since Lockdown began.

(NZ) Under Alert Level 2: we can get haircuts; go to the movies; see our mates; and go shopping. Schools are now open to all students. All shops are allowed to open, but there are restrictions on numbers. At restaurants and cafés all groups must be separated and have no more than ten people.

(NZ) Grant Robertson, the Finance Minister, has unveiled this years Budget, (a $50 Billion rescue fund), as the country braces for the economic carnage caused by Covid-19. The first $15.9 Billion includes an extension of the wage subsidy scheme to the hardest hit businesses, free trades training and a State House building program. Almost $14 Billion has already been allocated leaving $20 Billion still available. The New Zealand net public debt is projected to rise to 53.6% of Gross Domestic Product by 2023 and will leave the country in deficit for years to come. Grant Robertson says the pandemic is a 'one in a 100 year event' demanding record spending.

(NZ) For the third day running New Zealand has no new cases.

MAY 15 FRIDAY

(NZ) Today is the second day of Alert Level 2. It's been fifty-one days since Lockdown began.

(NZ) New Zealand has one new case today, associated with the Marist College cluster. The case has been described as a 'weak positive.' A weak positive usually means the test detected a very small amount of the virus. Various factors could affect the amount of virus that has been detected. It could be the stage of the illness at the time the sample was taken, or how well the sample was taken. Tests could also possibly be detecting left-over Covid-19 RNA from a virus that is dead. Whatever the reason today's 'weak positive' case is considered to be not infectious.

MAY 16 SATURDAY

(BANGLADESH) Bangladesh has the world's largest refugee settlement in the world. There are nearly a million people in this settlement and two people have tested positive for Covid-19.

(BRAZIL) Brazil has recently surged past Germany and France in Covid-19 cases. They have registered 218,223 cases and 14,817 deaths. In the last month Brazil has had two different health ministers. One was sacked; the other resigned.

(FRANCE) Health officials in France have drawn attention to the case of a 9 year-old boy who died a week ago after developing a syndrome similar to Kawasaki disease; this after being in contact with Covid-19. This syndrome has affected hundreds of children in Europe and America.

(NZ) Today is the third day of Alert Level 2. It's been fifty-two days since Lockdown began.

(NZ) In New Zealand, in the past 6 weeks, there have been at least 16 suspicious attacks on Cell Phone Towers. It's believed to be the work of Conspiracy Theorists who have linked the Covid-19 pandemic with the roll out of 5G wireless technology.

(NZ) There are no new cases in New Zealand today. 1428 of the 1498 cases have recovered. Three people are in hospital but none are in Intensive care.

MAY 17 SUNDAY

(BRAZIL) Brazil's cases have now passed Spain and Italy, making Brazil's Covid-19 outbreak the fourth largest in the world behind the United States, Russia, and the United Kingdom. Today Brazil had 14,919 new cases bringing their total to 233,142.

(CH) The Chinese city of Wuhan, where the Coronavirus pandemic began, has announced that it plans to test all of its 11 million residents for the virus. The plan was announced this week after Wuhan reported six cases after a month of not having any.

(NZ) Today is the fourth day of Alert Level 2. It's been fifty-three days since Lockdown began.

(NZ) There was another case of Covid-19 in New Zealand today. This case is related to the Rosewood cluster. There have been no further deaths. New Zealand now has a total of 1499 cases. 1433 people have recovered.

MAY 18 MONDAY

(NZ) Today is the fifth day of Alert Level 2. It's been fifty-four days since Lockdown began.

(NZ) 800,000 kids have gone back to school today. It appears that many of them, (and many of their parents), have been waiting for this day for some time.

(NZ) Prime Minister Jacinda Ardern announced that this week the Government would be releasing a contact-tracing app. She described it as a 'digital diary' that will help users log their movements. Work on a separate app using Bluetooth technology (like the one they have in Australia) is still under way. Whatever the app, there will be some people concerned about their privacy and how the gathered information is going to be used.

(NZ) According to a Reid Research Poll, Prime Minister Jacinda Ardern is the most popular New Zealand Prime Minister in a Century. The poll shows her as the most popular choice for leader at 59.5%. This is the highest any Prime Minister in New Zealand has ever scored. Simon Bridges, the leader of the opposition, scored 4.5%. The National Party has fallen to 30.6% under his leadership whereas Labour has risen to 56.5%.

(NZ) There were no new cases in New Zealand today. Yesterday 2570 tests were carried out. So far New Zealand has done a total of 230,718 tests since testing began.

(BRAZIL) Brazil's largest city, Sao Paulo, has said that its health system could collapse due to the growing demand for emergency beds.

MAY 19 TUESDAY

(BRAZIL) Brazil has overtaken the UK and is now the country with the third highest number of Covid-19 cases. Brazil has suffered 16,792 Covid-19 deaths, although under-reporting and low testing rates suggest that the true figure is likely to be much higher. There are images of cemetery workers digging countless graves. 38 indigenous groups in Brazil have been hit by the Coronavirus pandemic and at least 92 people have died. One of them is Messias Kokama, chief of the Parque das Tribos.

(NZ) Today is the sixth day of Alert Level 2. It's been fifty-five days since Lockdown began.

(NZ) Due to the decline in flight numbers caused by Covid-19, seven airports around New Zealand are to lose air traffic services They are: Hawkes Bay; Gisborne; New Plymouth; Rotorua; Invercargill; the Kapiti Coast Airport; and the Milford Sound Piopiotahi Aerodrome.

(NZ) There are no new cases in New Zealand but four cases have been reclassified as confirmed. These 4 relate to people who returned from the Greg Mortimer Cruise ship in Uruguay. Our new total is 1503. Of this total 1442 have recovered. That's 96%.

(US) The United States Food and Drug Administration (FDA) have released a document citing the side effects of hydroxychloroquine. They include: irreversible retinal damage, cardiac effects (including cardiomyopathy and QT prolongation), worsening of psoriasis and porphyria, proximal myopathy and neuropathy, neuropsychiatric events, and hypoglycaemia.

(US) President Trump says that he's been taking hydroxychloroquine to protect against Covid-19; this despite warnings that it is not effective and can damage the heart.

MAY 20 WEDNESDAY

(NZ) Today is the seventh day of Alert Level 2. It's been fifty-six days since Lockdown began.

(NZ) New Zealand's opposition party, the National Party, is in crisis and Simon Bridges is facing a leadership challenge. The challenge is coming from a man called Todd Muller. He's reportedly planning to challenge Bridges at a caucus meeting on Friday. New Zealand has an election coming up in September to determine who will govern the country. Due to their lack of popularity in the recent opinion polls the National Party has to do something.

(NZ) Air New Zealand has announced that it will be laying off 3500 personnel. 1300 cabin crew and 950 long and mid-haul crew, will lose their jobs. 300 workers are to be made redundant in Auckland, Wellington and Christchurch.

(NZ) 1500 jobs are on the line from Fletcher Building, New Zealand's largest construction company.

(NZ) There are no new cases today in New Zealand. In the last week there have been just two reported cases. The total sits at 1503.

MAY 21 THURSDAY

(GLOBAL) Coronavirus cases have passed 5 million. About 2 weeks ago it was (only) 4 million. Numbers seem to be jumping up a million every fortnight. Over 330 thousand people around the world have died. Over 2 million people have recovered.

April 2 (1 million cases)
April 15 (2 million cases)
April 27 (3 million cases)
May 8 (4 million cases)
May 21 (5 million cases)

(COVID-19) The New Normal.

Although the phrase has been around for some time it's been firmly attached to the Covid-19 crisis. In the Covid-19 context, because there is no cure for the virus, the new normal suggests that we may have to adjust to a new way of living and going about our everyday lives. We may have to change the way we interact with other people and we may have to accept that some things are gone. We are already affected by Covid-19 so there's been a great deal of change already. The 'new normal' will be determined mostly by how society fits in with a world affected by Covid-19.

(NZ) Today is the eighth day of Alert Level 2. It's been fifty-seven days since Lockdown began.

(NZ) Pubs across New Zealand are allowed to open today as long as they restrict numbers to 100, and ensure their customers are seated, separated, and served at their table. There is a ban on dancing, which means that many late night venues will remain closed for now.

(NZ) 250,000 people in New Zealand have so far downloaded the Contact Tracing app released by the Ministry of Health. There have been complaints that the app does not work on older cell phones, and that it's insufficient for business needs. At the moment the NZ Covid-19 Tracker only does two things. It scans QR codes from participating businesses, and it allows you to send some personal info to the Ministry of Health, if you want to. There are plans to add updates at a later stage.

(NZ) New Zealand has had its fourth consecutive day of zero cases of Covid-19.

MAY 22 FRIDAY

(NZ) Today is the ninth day of Alert Level 2. It's been fifty-eight days since Lockdown began.

(NZ) Simon Bridges has been ousted as the leader of New Zealand's National Party, replaced by Todd Muller. Mr Muller says that he expects to be Prime Minister come the September election. He concedes that the present Government's handling of the Covid-19 pandemic has been 'impressive' but says it's time to rebuild the country, and only National can do that.

(NZ) There are 43,000 more people on the Jobseeker Support Benefit than there was before the Lockdown in late March. $10.9 Billion has been paid out so far from the Government's wage subsidy scheme for businesses.

(NZ) New Zealand has one new case today. It's the first new case in five days. It's a household contact case associated with the St Margaret's cluster. The total number of cases in New Zealand is now 1504.

MAY 23 SATURDAY

(WHO) The World Health Organisation has declared South America the 'new epicentre' of the pandemic.

(AUS) Because of injuries and the restrictions on getting replacement players from New Zealand, the NRL (Australia's National Rugby League Competition) have allowed the New Zealand Warriors to loan players from rival Australian clubs.

(BRAZIL) Brazil has overtaken Russia as the country with the second highest number of Coronavirus cases; behind the United States. Brazil has recorded 330,890 cases and 21,048 deaths, though experts have consistently said that under-testing means that the real figures could be 15 times higher than that. Brazil's death toll is currently the sixth highest in the world behind the US, Britain, Italy, Spain, and France.

(NZ) Today is the tenth day of Alert Level 2. It's been fifty-nine days since Lockdown began.

(NZ) A New Zealand company is going to attempt to develop a Covid-19 vaccine. They are about to start pulling in experts from around the country. If successful they have said that it would provide more security for the New Zealand population.

(NZ) There are no new cases today in New Zealand. The total number of people who have been tested in NZ has now passed 250,000.

(RUSSIA) Russia has registered 326,488 cases with 3200 deaths.

(US) The United States has registered more than 1.6 million cases and nearly 96,000 deaths.

MAY 24 SUNDAY

(NZ) Today is the eleventh day of Alert Level 2. It's been sixty days since Lockdown began.

(NZ) The New Zealand Government is removing the requirement for building consents on low-risk building work, such as sleep-outs, sheds, or carports. This is an effort to let the construction sector work on larger projects and assist the Covid-19 recovery.

(NZ) The sequels to the Avatar movie may be able to resume filming in New Zealand. The producer, Jon Landau, has said that as New Zealand has handled the Covid-19 crisis pretty well he has no qualms about coming back to New Zealand with a small crew. Weta Digital and Lightstorm VFX teams have been able to work from home.

(NZ) Two pubs in Auckland have been shut down for failing to comply with restrictions under Alert Level Two.

(NZ) There are no new cases in New Zealand today. This is the second day in a row. There have been only three cases in the last 13 days. The total remains at 1504. The number of people who have recovered is 1456. That's 97%.

MAY 25 MONDAY

(AUS) The Australian Government is pushing ahead with the arrangement to open its borders to New Zealand despite Queensland's insistence on keeping strict Covid-19 border controls in place.

(NZ) Today is the twelfth day of Alert Level 2. It's been sixty-one days since Lockdown began.

(NZ) Prime Minister Jacinda Ardern has implied that New Zealanders might not have to wait until Alert Level 1 to travel to Australia.

(NZ) Prime Minister Jacinda Ardern has announced that from midday this Friday gatherings of up to 100 people will be allowed under Alert Level 2. She says that the increased numbers are possible because there have been no new cases attributable to the relaxed restrictions brought in as we stepped down into Level 3, more than three weeks ago. She says that New Zealand will remain at Level 2 for at least four more weeks. Dr Ashley Bloomfield says that restrictions in New Zealand are already being relaxed faster than those in neighbouring countries such as Australia.

(NZ) Finance Minister Grant Robertson has introduced a new 12-week relief payment scheme for New Zealand citizens and residents. It will come into effect on the 8th of June paying $490 to those who have lost full-time work, and $250 for part-time workers including students.

(NZ) There are no new cases of Covid-19 today. There have been only 3 cases in the last fortnight. One person remains in hospital.

(US) In the US 98,218 people have died of Covid-19. This is more than the number of US troops killed in the Korean and Vietnam wars combined.

(US) It's the end of the Memorial Day weekend in the US and crowds have packed beaches in Florida, Maryland, Georgia, Virginia, and Indiana. Not many were wearing masks or practicing social distancing. In Missouri hundreds have attended a pool party, just days after a similar party in Arkansas caused a cluster of new cases. Arkansas is experiencing a second peak.

(US) President Trump has suspended travel into the United States for people who have been to Brazil within the past two weeks.

MAY 26 TUESDAY

(AUS) Two schools in Sydney have been closed after students tested positive for Covid-19. Sydney only allowed their students to return full-time to their classrooms yesterday.

(NZ) Today is the thirteenth day of Alert Level 2. It's been sixty-two days since Lockdown began.

(NZ) Around 100 different vaccines are being developed around the world and New Zealand is taking part in that development. Dr Ashley Bloomfield believes it will be 12-18 months before a vaccine is available for the public. This is more than enough time for the anti-vaxxers to start spreading their propaganda.

(NZ) Covid-19 has had an impact on the global price of potatoes. There is a mountain of product sitting in European cool stores that are going nowhere. This could impact the potato industry in New Zealand. There are calls to ban frozen potato fries from European producers, who could be eyeing up world markets to dump their surplus product.

(NZ) There are no new cases in New Zealand today. The total remains at 1504.

MAY 27 WEDNESDAY

(NZ) Today is the fourteenth day of Alert Level 2. It's been sixty-three days since Lockdown began.

(NZ) Deputy Prime Minister Winston Peters says he is frustrated at the speed at which the Government is heading towards Alert Level One. He believes we should be there now.

(NZ) New Zealand had 31 new cases in the 16 days of Alert Level 3 and so far there has been only 3 new cases in the 14 days of Alert Level 2. There are no new cases today. This makes it 5 days in a row.

(US) There's footage on the News of a white Policeman in Minneapolis, Derek Chauvin, with his knee pressing into the neck of a black man called George Floyd. Mr Floyd calls out multiple times that he can't breathe. He was rushed to hospital but died on Monday night. The four officers involved in his arrest were fired on Tuesday. The Minneapolis Mayer has called for Derek Chauvin to be criminally charged. Because of the public outrage there have been protests spreading across the United States. Angry crowds in Minneapolis are setting fire and looting stores and causing damage that has stretched for miles.

MAY 28 THURSDAY

(WHO) Since early March, across 24 European countries, there have been more than 159,000 excess deaths. These are deaths above and beyond the number of 'normally expected' deaths for the same period of time.

(AUS) The NRL (Australia's National Rugby League) has become the first professional sporting competition to restart in Australia. In Brisbane, the Parramatta Eels played the Brisbane Broncos. No supporters were permitted inside the Stadium. Virtual crowd noises were added to the live-television broadcast to create the impression of a live crowd.

(HONG KONG) There have been riots in Hong Kong over controversial legislation aimed at bringing the territory further under Beijing's control.

(NZ) Today is the fifteenth day of Alert Level 2. It's been sixty-four days since Lockdown began.

(NZ) Regarding the Trans-Tasman bubble, Prime Minister Jacinda Ardern says that September could be a realistic time frame for New Zealand's borders to open up to Australia.

(NZ) 37,500 people became unemployed in April. In recent weeks there have been major lay offs by big companies such as Air New Zealand, Fletcher Building, Sky City, and Millennium and Copthorne Hotels.

(NZ) There are no new cases in New Zealand today. This is the sixth day in a row. There are still 8 active cases. We have no more hospital cases as the last person has been discharged. The number of deaths has gone up one as a lady in her 90s, from St Margaret's Rest Home, died on Sunday after being considered recovered from Covid-19. The New Zealand death toll is now 22.

(US) Rioting continues in Minneapolis over the killing of George Floyd by a Police Officer.

(US) The US has hit 100,000 Covid-19 deaths. President Trump has tweeted that the figure is 'a very sad milestone.'

(US) 40 million Americans have filed for unemployment benefits since March. This is the equivalent of one in four American workers. More than 2 million of those claims were made last week.

MAY 29 FRIDAY

(NZ) Today is the sixteenth day of Alert Level 2. It's been sixty-five days since Lockdown began.

(NZ) From midday groups of up to 100 people will be allowed in New Zealand. The rules of 'seated, separated, and single server,' still apply for hospitality businesses but they can now take group bookings of more than 10 people.

(NZ) It's been a week since New Zealand had its last Covid-19 case. There are no further cases today. The total number of cases remains at 1504 and New Zealand now has only one active case left. 7 people have recovered since yesterday.

(S KOREA) South Korea has had their biggest jump in Covid-19 cases in fifty days. Yesterday there were 58 new cases alone. 200 schools have been closed with students returning to online lessons. South Korea's situation is seen as an example that Covid-19 is particularly hard to defeat, and countries shouldn't rejoice too early with their low case numbers.

(US) Riots continue in the city of Minneapolis where a white policeman killed George Floyd, a black man. The Police Department in Minneapolis has been torched while in Detroit a 21 year-old man has been shot. President Trump has called the protesters 'thugs' tweeting that 'when the looting starts, the shooting starts.' Twitter has said that this violates its rules against promoting violence. The Police Officer who killed George Floyd, a white man called Derek Chauvin, has been arrested and charged with third-degree murder and second-degree manslaughter. Under Minnesota law, third-degree murder is defined as causing death of a person 'by perpetrating an act eminently dangerous to others and evincing a depraved mind,' without regard for life and without intent to kill. Under Minnesota law, a person is guilty of second-degree manslaughter when that person recklessly causes the death of another person, also without an intent to kill.

MAY 30 SATURDAY

(NZ) Today is the seventeenth day of Alert Level 2. It's been sixty-six days since Lockdown began.

(NZ) In New Zealand it's the start of the Queen's Birthday Weekend holiday. After weeks of restrictions New Zealanders are able to travel away for their first long weekend since Lockdown began in late March. Those who missed out at Easter are taking advantage of the extra day. Many are also taking advantage of a $29-a-day campervan deal from Tourism Holdings Ltd. As Kiwis can't travel overseas anymore this is an attempt to get New Zealanders to see their own country. The $29 deal is in place until the end of October.

(NZ) As New Zealand has only one active case of Covid-19 and there hasn't been a new case in over a week, a lot of the community testing centres are closing down. People wanting tests will have to go to their GP.

(NZ) Sir David Skegg, a New Zealand epidemiologist, has stated that people who 'advocate a move to Level One straight away are either ignorant or indulging in political posturing.' Deputy Prime Minister Winston Peters has been calling for us to go to Level One, as has the new National Party leader, Todd Muller.

(UK) The UK has adjusted their death toll to include deaths in all settings, not just hospitals. Their numbers have shot up by almost 8000 people, rising from 30,861 to 38,489.

(US) 12 States, including Minnesota, have called up the National Guard to help deal with the ongoing protests against Police Brutality and the death of George Floyd. At least 25 cities have imposed curfews. In Washington DC the National Guard are assisting Police outside the White House, which has been placed in Lockdown due to protesters outside. Looters have ransacked stores in Melrose Avenue in Los Angeles. In Philadelphia protesters have defied curfew and set buildings on fire. In Atlanta the CNN Center has been targeted.

MAY 31 SUNDAY

(GLOBAL) While demonstrators are defying curfew in many US states there are other countries around the world holding demonstrations against Police Brutality and the death of George Floyd. There have been protests in London, Berlin, Copenhagen, Rio de Janeiro, and Vancouver.

(NZ) Today is the eighteenth day of Alert Level 2. It's been sixty-seven days since Lockdown began.

(NZ) This is the 9th day without a new case of Covid-19. New Zealand still has one active case. The person is recovering at home.

(US) A rocket ship designed and built by Elon Musk's SpaceX Company has lifted off from Cape Canaveral in Florida with two Astronauts on board. It is the first time in nearly a decade that NASA has launched Astronauts from US soil. Their destination is the International Space Station, 250 miles above the Earth.

(GLOBAL) 221 countries and territories have had cases of the Coronavirus. In May, South Ossetia, and Lesotho reported their first cases.

(GLOBAL) The following 10 countries and territories reported their first cases in April: Caribbean Netherlands; Comoros; Falkland Islands; Malawi; Saint Pierre Miquelon; Sao Tome and Principe; South Sudan; Tajikistan; Western Sahara; and Yemen.

(GLOBAL) The following 138 countries and territories reported their first cases in March: Albania; Andorra; Angola; Anguilla; Antigua and Barbuda; Argentina; Armenia; Aruba; Bahamas; Bangladesh; Barbados; Belize; Benin; Bermuda; Bhutan; Bolivia; Bosnia and Herzegovina; Botswana; British Virgin

Islands; Brunei; Bulgaria; Burkina Faso; Burundi; Cabo Verde; Cameroon; Cayman Islands; Central African Republic; Chad; Channel Islands; Chile; Colombia; Congo; Costa Rica; Cuba; Curaçao; Cyprus; Czech Republic; DR Congo; Djibouti; Dominican Republic; El Salvador; Equatorial Guinea; Eritrea; Eswatini; Ethiopia; Faroe Islands; Fiji; French Guinea; French Polynesia; Gabon; Gambia; Ghana; Gibraltar; Greenland; Grenada; Guadalupe; Guam; Guatemala; Guinea; Guinea-Bissau; Guyana; Haiti; Honduras; Hungary; Indonesia; Isle Of Man; Ivory Coast; Jamaica; Jordan; Kazakhstan; Kenya; Kyrgyzstan; Laos; Latvia; Liberia; Libya; Liechtenstein; Madagascar; Maldives; Mali; Malta; Martinique; Mauritania; Mauritius; Mayotte; Moldova; Mongolia; Montenegro; Montserrat; Morocco; Mozambique; Myanmar; Namibia; New Caledonia; Nicaragua; Niger; Palestine; Panama; Papua New Guinea; Paraguay; Peru; Poland; Portugal; Réunion; Rwanda; Saudi Arabia; St Barth; Saint Kitts and Nevis; Saint Lucia; Saint Martin; St Vincent and the Grenadines; Senegal; Serbia; Seychelles; Sierra Leone; Sint Maaten; Slovakia; Slovenia; Somalia; South Africa; Sudan; Suriname; Syria; Tanzania; Timor-Leste; Togo; Trinidad and Tobago; Tunisia; Turkey; Turks and Caicos Islands; Uganda; Ukraine; Uruguay; Uzbekistan; Vatican City; Venezuela; Zambia; and Zimbabwe.

(GLOBAL) The following 35 countries and territories reported their first cases in February: Algeria; Austria; Azerbaijan; Bahrain; Belarus; Belgium; Croatia; Denmark; Egypt; Ecuador; Estonia; Georgia; Greece; Iceland; Iran; Iraq; Ireland; Israel, Kuwait; Lebanon; Lithuania; Luxembourg; Mexico; Monaco; the Netherlands; New Zealand; Nigeria; North Macedonia; Norway; Oman; Pakistan; Qatar; Romania; San Marino; and Switzerland.

(GLOBAL) The following 27 countries and territories reported their first cases in January, (or earlier in the case of China): Australia; Cambodia; Canada; China; Finland; France; Germany; Hong Kong; India; Italy; Japan; Macau; Malaysia; Nepal; Philippines; Russia; Singapore; Spain; Sweden; South Korea; Sri Lanka; Taiwan; Thailand; the United Arab Emirates; the United Kingdom; the United States of America; and Vietnam.

(GLOBAL) There are still Countries and territories that have not had (or reported) any cases of Coronavirus. Most of the following are isolated island nations in the Pacific Ocean: American Samoa; Ascension; Christmas Island; Cocos Islands, Cook Islands; Federated States of Micronesia; Kiribati; Marshall Islands; Nauru; Niue; Norfolk Island; North Korea; Palau; Pitcairn Islands; Saint Helena; Sahrawi Arab Democratic Republic; Samoa; Solomon Islands; Svalbard; Tokelau; Tonga; Tristan da Cunha; Turkmenistan; Tuvalu; Vanuatu; and, Wallis and Futuna.

(ANTARCTICA) Antarctica is the only Continent in the world with no cases of Covid-19.

MAY: NEW ZEALAND AND AUSTRALIA

Towards the end of our Alert Level 4 Lockdown there were many people complaining that the restrictions had been too harsh and that New Zealand had gone 'Too Hard,' in their "Go Early and Go Hard" approach to combatting Covid-19.

They were saying that we should have been more like Australia, who, without putting the whole nation into Lockdown, was showing similar rates of cases per capita as New Zealand. In Australia you could still get a haircut, go to a liquor outlet, and get takeaway coffee, whereas in New Zealand you couldn't do any of these things; and a lot more.

Now it's obvious that Australia has done a great job keeping their case numbers down, but the idea of us changing what we're doing to copy them seems ridiculous considering that we're doing so well by ourselves. Yes, we can learn from another country's success, but you shouldn't rearrange your game plan if it's working. And as everyone has discovered, there's no handbook for dealing with Covid-19.

So, Australia is doing well. That's great. Excellent.

So many countries aren't doing so well. These are the ones that we should be taking notice of if we are looking at eliminating the virus. We have to continue to learn from these countries because Covid-19 is a sneaky bastard that, like a liquid, will exploit any hole. And when it gets through it quickly becomes an inundation. Countries that are easing their Lockdown restrictions too fast are paying the price with new cases surging.

Australia, (and a lot of other countries), has opted for 'containment' as their chosen response to the Covid-19 pandemic. (Containment means that the virus is there but it's under control). New Zealand on the other hand has decided on elimination; therefore the rules have to be a lot harsher. It's totally understandable that people would wish that we had the same level of freedom as our neighbours across the Tasman, but if you're going for elimination then you can't mess around, and you can't be tempted by what might be working for countries that are aiming at containment. To eliminate you have to 'Go Hard,' and take no prisoners.

How Australia was achieving their excellent results was confusing, as it seemed to be going against all the theories related to the spread of viruses. But I had a theory. And it goes back to the bushfires and the purchasing of toilet paper.

Now my theory is my own and it's probably totally wrong, maybe even controversial, but I'm sure there would be at least a few Aussies that could back it up.

My theory as to why Australia's case numbers were on a par with us in New Zealand was that a lot of Australians were acting the same way as we were. I'm not saying that they were looking at our country and thinking that we should be emulated, no, not at all. I believe that a lot of Australians, (like us), were looking at other countries that were failing badly, and had decided to personally not let that happen to them, and their family. The Australian people didn't need a Government to tell them to self-isolate. I reckon a lot of them just did it themselves. They weren't out in the community doing their shopping because they'd already done it. Those panic-buying toilet-paper-people we laughed at were examples of Australians getting ready to go into hiding. I believe that Supermarket shelves ran empty because Australians were buying up large and getting prepared to stay at home. And like us in New Zealand, if you stayed at home then you didn't catch, or spread, the virus. And if the population wasn't out there catching or spreading the virus, then naturally the case numbers remained low.

So how does this fit in with the bushfires? Well... the way that the Australian Government dealt with the bushfire crisis was heavily criticised. To make matters worse the Prime Minister took his family on a holiday to Hawaii while vast areas of the country were still burning. People remember that at a time when the country needed their leader he was on holiday. A lot of people must have lost faith in their leader and his Government's response to the bushfires, and if you lose faith in how one disaster is handled, then maybe you're not so confident in how another one is going to be dealt with.

My theory is that a lot of Australian's took it upon themselves to self-isolate, and that was what kept the numbers down.

But it's only a theory, and like all theories, until proven correct they're all just wind. (And I'm not particularly bothered if it's proven correct or not. I'm just happy that Australia's knocking it back).

The New Zealand Government has proven that it listens to what the New Zealand public has to say and debates the merits of a lot of things that are suggested. Sometimes they change their policies, sometimes not. That they didn't buckle under the pressure to open businesses showed a certain backbone that I think might be lacking in a lot of Governments around the world, where industry giants or voters sway the direction of a Government's thinking.

In September, New Zealand will be holding its elections to see who governs the country for the next three years. Whether the New Zealand public votes for a party that chose to protect the health of the population over the impact of the country's economy, will be determined when New Zealanders go to the voting booths on September 19.

Jason Komene 6 June 2020

JUNE 2020

JUNE 1 MONDAY

(GLOBAL) More than 6 million people worldwide have been infected with Covid-19. The global death toll has surpassed 370,000 people.

> **April 2 (1 million cases)**
> **April 15 (2 million cases)**
> **April 27 (3 million cases)**
> **May 8 (4 million cases)**
> **May 21 (5 million cases)**
> **June 1 (6 million cases)**

(GLOBAL) There are Black Lives Matter demonstrations in Paris, Mexico City, Dublin, and Perth.

(PHILIPPINES) Authorities are easing Lockdown restrictions in Manila. Public transport is running with a limited number of passengers. Thousands of people will be able to return to work.

(NZ) Today is the 19th day of Alert Level 2. It's been sixty-eight days since Lockdown began.

(NZ) New Zealand has joined the worldwide demonstrations over the death of George Floyd with protests in Auckland and Christchurch and a vigil in Wellington. Footage of the demonstrations show crowds in the thousands. New Zealand is at Alert Level Two, which only allows for groups up to 100 people. There were about 4000 people at the Auckland rally. A few people are wearing masks but it's clear that for the demonstrations Social Distancing protocols have gone out the window.

(NZ) 56 film workers, including James Cameron and Avatar

producer Jon Landau, have flown into Wellington on a specially chartered flight. They are being quarantined at the QT Hotel in Wellington for the next 14 days.

(NZ) It is the 10th day without a new case of Covid-19. There is still one active case. New Zealand is on the brink of becoming the first country in the world that was significantly affected by Covid-19 (1504 cases), to eliminate all cases. An Otago University Study suggests that eradication may be possible in NZ, with 95% certainty, around the third week of June.

JUNE 2 TUESDAY

(CANADA) Canadian Prime Minister Justin Trudeau drew attention to himself today after being asked a question on how he felt President Trump was handling George Floyd protesters. His answer came after a painful 20 seconds of silence, where the Prime Minister seemed to be considering how best to answer such a question. In the end he didn't actually address the question but instead focussed on racial inequalities in Canada.

(FRANCE) France is allowing restaurants, bars, and beaches to reopen. In 'green' areas where the virus circulates slowly, the only limit will be a minimum of 1 metre between tables. In 'orange' areas bars, restaurants and cafés will only be permitted to open their outdoor terraces.

(HONG KONG) A new cluster in Hong Kong has emerged after two weeks of zero cases. It is connected to a warehouse with no clear overseas source.

(ITALY) Italy has reopened to travellers from Europe. Italy was the first European country to be hit hard by the Coronavirus and for a time was the epicentre for Covid-19. They have had more than 33,000 deaths. Italy is still reporting dozens of new cases a day.

(NZ) Today is the 20th day of Alert Level 2. It's been sixty-nine days since Lockdown began.

(NZ) Prime Minister Jacinda Ardern has admitted that New Zealand could possibly go to Alert Level One as early as next week, if there are no further unexpected cases. She was asked if the lack of enforcement of Level Two rules, at yesterday's marches, meant that the Government had lost its authority to determine the rules. She replied that it was up to the Police to

determine how to enforce the rules. 'Some rules were broken in Alert Level 4. That's no reason for us to abandon restrictions that have been put in place for the health and safety of all New Zealanders.'

(NZ) To aid the Covid-19 recovery there is going to be a 'Targeted Training and Apprenticeship Fund,' (TTAF), that will cover the costs of learners of all ages undertaking vocational education and training. The fund will target training that will give learners better employment prospects. Apprentices working in all industries will have their costs paid. Starting on the 1st of July the Government will be targeting programs in: Construction, Primary Industries (agriculture, horticulture, fisheries etc.), Community Support (Elderly care, youth work, counselling etc.), Manufacturing and Mechanical Engineering, Electrical Engineering, and Road Transport (e.g. Heavy Vehicle Operators).

(NZ) There are no new cases in NZ. This is the 11th day in a row.

JUNE 3 WEDNESDAY

(NZ) Today is the 21st day of Alert Level 2. It's been seventy days since Lockdown began.

(NZ) Director-General of Health, Ashley Bloomfield, has said that since there is currently no evidence of community transmission in NZ, quarantining for 14 days after attending one of the outdoor protests is not required. He has asked for people to be kind to those who have recovered from the virus, saying that there should be no stigma attached to having had the disease.

(NZ) Prime Minister Jacinda Ardern says that under Alert Level 1 there will still be strict controls on the border, but all current rules and restrictions related to businesses and services will be essentially lifted. There will also be an end to restrictions for hospitality businesses, and gatherings. Funerals and Tangihanga of any size will be able to take place. Physical distancing would not be necessary and community sport can start again. Contact tracing efforts will remain in place.

(NZ) Today is the 12th day with no new cases in New Zealand.

(SPAIN) Spain has extended its State of Emergency to June 21.

JUNE 4 THURSDAY

(BRAZIL) Brazil has registered 1473 Covid-19 deaths in a 24-hour period. That's an average of one every 58 seconds.

(COOK ISLANDS) The Cook Islands want New Zealand tourists to visit as soon as New Zealand enters Alert Level 1. Henry Puna, the Cook Islands Prime Minister, says that as there is no community transmission in NZ there's no risk and the Cook Islands should be treated as a domestic flight. The Cook Islands have not had any cases of Covid-19.

(JORDAN) Jordan has reopened its mosques for the first time in over two months. Worshippers are asked to wear facemasks and keep a safe distance from their neighbours. From tomorrow cafés and hotels can reopen and domestic flights will resume. Schools, universities and cinemas will remain closed and most public gatherings are still banned.

(NZ) Today is the 22nd day of Alert Level 2. It's been seventy-one days since Lockdown began.

(NZ) It is now 13 days with no new Covid-19 cases. There is still one active case left.

(US) Hundreds of people have gathered in a Minneapolis chapel to remember George Floyd who died at the hands of a Police Officer on May 25. It is the first of several memorials being held in different cities over the next few days. Marches are continuing all over the United States, and the world.

(US) The United States have almost 2 million Covid-19 cases. (1,940,315). 22,819 people have tested positive in the United States today. With all of the demonstrations across the country it's unlikely that the daily count will go down in a hurry.

JUNE 5 FRIDAY

(NZ) Today is the 23rd day of Alert Level 2. It's been seventy-two days since Lockdown began.

(NZ) It has now been a fortnight of no new Cases of Covid-19 in New Zealand.

JUNE 6 SATURDAY

(WHO) The World Health Organisation has emphasized that masks should be part of a comprehensive strategy in the fight against Covid-19. Where physical distancing is difficult (e.g. public transport, shops etc.), the public is advised to wear masks.

(AUS) The Police in Sydney won a court ruling with the New South Wales supreme court, saying that the Black Lives Matter protest planned for today would be unlawful under Covid-19 restrictions. Despite this, protesters vowed to go ahead with the Sydney rally. Thousands gathered outside Town Hall half an hour before the protest was due to start, where the Organisers of the rally lodged a last-ditch appeal. After a late decision by the Court of Appeal the rally was declared an authorised public assembly. The decision came minutes before the rally's scheduled start at 3PM.

(NZ) Today is the 24th day of Alert Level 2. It's been seventy-three days since Lockdown began.

(NZ) The Royal New Zealand College of General Practitioners has stated that we were literally a week away from not being able to contain the virus when the decision was made to go into Lockdown. We were staring down the barrel of a potential health system meltdown, similar to those seen in Italy, Spain, the UK, and the United States.

(NZ) New Zealand has completed 291,994 tests to date. 3007 tests were performed yesterday.

JUNE 7 SUNDAY

(LATIN AMERICA) Latin America has nearly 1.2 million cases and more than 60,000 deaths. These numbers are likely to be less than the true total as several countries don't do as many tests as others, and a lot of Covid-19 deaths go unreported.

(BRAZIL) Brazil is likely to see 1 million cases and 50,000 deaths by June 20, but tracking total numbers is going to be difficult from now on as President Jair Bolsonaro's Government has stopped reporting total numbers. It will only report new cases and deaths each day.

(CH) China has issued a travel warning to its citizens to not travel to Australia. This is due to what they say is a spike in racist attacks towards Chinese and Asian people over the Covid-19 crisis.

(NZ) Today is the 25th day of Alert Level 2. It's been seventy-four days since Lockdown began.

(US) The United States has recorded over 2 million Covid-19 cases, (2,007,449). 112,469 people have died from Covid-19.

JUNE 8 MONDAY

(GLOBAL) The number of international cases has reached 7 million. There were 6 million cases a week ago. This is the fastest rise of a million cases since the pandemic began.

April 2 (1 million cases)
April 15 (2 million cases)
April 27 (3 million cases)
May 8 (4 million cases)
May 21 (5 million cases)
June 1 (6 million cases)
June 8 (7 million cases)

(C-19) Lockdowns, social distancing, travel restrictions and other interventions, may have prevented half a billion Covid-19 infections in six countries (including China and the US). Most interventions took three weeks to achieve full impact.

(INDIA) In India, malls, restaurants and places of worship have reopened despite a spike in new infections.

(NZ) Today is the 22nd day of Alert Level 2. It's been seventy-five days since Lockdown began, and today New Zealand no longer has any active cases of Covid-19. This is the first time since February that we've been free of Covid-19. Prime Minister Jacinda Ardern admits that she did a little dance with her daughter, but was reluctant to repeat the dance for the general public.

(NZ) Ashley Bloomfield paid tribute to health workers and essential workers, adding that the achievement had come because 'New Zealanders acted together in our collective interests.' Concerning whether we should have come down to Alert

Level One faster, he said that: 'we have come down faster and sooner and in a stronger position than any other country. Yes we have been cautious, but we have not been over-cautious.'

(NZ) At 11:59 PM tonight New Zealand will be moving down to Alert Level 1. This removes all remaining restrictions except for controls at the border.

(TANZANIA) The President of Tanzania has declared the country Covid-19 free. He says that: 'The Corona disease has been eliminated thanks to God.' The World Health Organisation has expressed concern over the Government's Covid-19 strategy. The last official data was released on April 29.

(US) After 100 days since their first case was confirmed, New York City is slowly reopening. Nearly 400,000 people are expected to return to retail stores, factories, and construction sites.

JUNE 9 TUESDAY

(GLOBAL) New Zealand joins eight other countries that had Covid-19 infections but now report zero active cases. Montenegro, Eritrea, Papua New Guinea, Seychelles, Vatican City, Saint Kitts and Nevis, Fiji, and East Timor.

(BRAZIL) Because of an uproar, a Supreme Court Judge has ordered the Government to resume the release of Covid-19 cases and deaths. The Government had planned to stop recording figures after the weekend. Now amid accusations of censorship and data manipulation they will resume reporting Coronavirus figures.

(NZ) New Zealand has no more active cases. The last community-based transmission was on May 1st, 39 days ago. It's been 18 days since the last reported case.

(NZ) New Zealand is at Alert Level One. This means that except for Border Controls we are now free of all the restrictions we lived under during all the other Alert Levels. We can gather in masses and pretty much go about our lives like we did before Covid-19 came along.

(NZ) Here is a list of the number of Covid-19 cases reported by District Health Boards around New Zealand.

> Auckland (178)
> Bay Of Plenty (47)
> Canterbury (164)
> Capital and Coast (95)
> Counties (132)
> Hawkes Bay (44)
> Hutt Valley (20)
> Lakes (16)

Mid Central (32)
Nelson Marlborough (49)
Northland (28)
South Canterbury (17)
Southern (216)
Tairāwhiti (4)
Taranaki (16)
Waikato (188)
Wairarapa (8)
Waitemata (236)
West Coast (5)
Whanganui(9)

(NZ) No cases have been reported on either Stewart Island or the Chatham Islands.

(US) The funeral for George Floyd took place today in Houston, Texas. About 500 guests, (all wearing face masks), attended the service. After the service a hearse, followed by his family and given a police escort, carried Mr Floyd's golden casket to the cemetery. The last mile of the journey to his resting place was in a horse drawn carriage.

JUNE 10 WEDNESDAY

(LIBYA) Covid-19 cases have surged in Libya and health authorities are blaming the repatriation of nationals stranded abroad. At present there is no quarantine for repatriated Libyans.

(NZ) New Zealand has no more active cases. The last community-based transmission was 40 days ago. It's been 19 days since the last reported case.

(NZ) Air New Zealand has been under fire for refusing to refund people for cancelled flights. After a massive decline in revenue resulting from the Covid-19 crisis the airline received a $900 million lifeline from the New Zealand Government, as well as $70 million in wage subsidies. They have cut more than 4000 jobs and there are more on the line. According to their chief revenue officer, Cam Wallace, they have a compassionate policy where people can ring in about their unique financial hardship and perhaps claim a refund. Already they've refunded 15,000 individual cases. This averages out to about $20 million dollars a week.

(NZ) Prime Minister Jacinda Ardern has expressed anger over the 'Warehouse' Group's plans to cut 1080 jobs. She says she gets hundreds of letters from small businesses doing everything they can to keep their employees. She said she'd like to see the same attitude applied by some of our large organisations in New Zealand. The Finance spokesman for the opposition party, (the National Party), has said that: "she should stick to her knitting." This comment has been labelled sexist by some, and hasn't particularly endeared the National Party to younger people who are not familiar with the phrase.

(SWEDEN) Sweden has recorded 46,814 cases and 4795

deaths from Covid-19. Sweden was criticised by many countries for following a 'herd immunity' Covid-19 response. 90% of their deaths have occurred among the over-70s; half were in care homes. In contrast, deaths in the other Scandinavian countries, (Denmark, Norway, and Finland), numbered in the low hundreds.

(US) In the US, 22 States are showing a downward trend in Coronavirus cases. 9 are holding steady, while 19 States still have increasing cases. These 19 States are: Alaska, Arizona, Arkansas, Florida, Georgia, Hawaii, Kentucky, Michigan, Nevada, New Mexico, North Carolina, North Dakota, Oklahoma, Oregon, South Carolina, South Dakota, Utah, Vermont, and Washington.

JUNE 11 THURSDAY

(BRAZIL) Brazil has the second highest number of cases in the world with 772,416.

(NZ) New Zealand has no more active cases. The last community-based transmission was 41 days ago. It's been 20 days since the last reported case.

(NZ) All around the world major sporting competitions are being played before empty stadiums, (or stadiums stacked with cardboard cut-outs in the stands). Taiwan has had Baseball matches with crowd numbers limited to 1000 people. This Saturday, in Dunedin, there will be a match between two New Zealand Rugby teams as the Super Rugby Aotearoa competition begins. (The Super Rugby competition used to consist of teams from Argentina, Australia, Japan, New Zealand, and South Africa; until Covid-19 came along and caused border closures). Saturday's match is The Highlanders vs. The Chiefs. It is expected that all of the seats of the 22,800-capacity Stadium will sell out, making it the first full Stadium match of anything in the world from a country that has been hit by Covid-19.

(NZ) There are reports that guests from different flights are mingling at Auckland's Crowne Plaza Hotel where they are under a 14-day quarantine; so it's not unusual for a person on their 14th day at the hotel to mingle with someone who has just flown in. It's said that some people have even had outside guests come in and visit the hotel. There's footage on the 6 O'clock News of guests being chaperoned as they take their daily walk amongst unsuspecting members of the public. None of them are wearing masks. One guest has said that he feels more exposed to the Covid-19 virus in his hotel than he did the whole time he was in the Philippines.

(RUSSIA) Russia has passed 500,000 Covid-19 cases.

(US) The United States has passed two million cases of Covid-19. They listed 2,000,464 cases.

JUNE 12 FRIDAY

(GLOBAL) In recent weeks some States in the US, and many countries around the world, have started relaxing lockdown restrictions. Because of the Black Lives Matter protests that have erupted almost everywhere, there are fears that the number of new cases will spike.

(INDIA) India has overtaken the UK to become the fourth worst hit nation, behind the US, Brazil, and Russia.

(NZ) New Zealand has no more active cases. The last community-based transmission was 42 days ago. It's been 21 days since the last reported case.

(NZ) Because of weeks of Lockdown in New Zealand there was a halt put on a feral chicken removal project in Titirangi. Caring locals fed the birds during their daily walks and now the feral chicken population of Titirangi has exploded. News of this phenomenon has gone global. Horror Writer Stephen King has tweeted: "The chickens came out of the shadows... WITH A THIRST FOR VENGEANCE."

JUNE 13 SATURDAY

(GLOBAL) In the United States and around the world statues of historical figures have come under attack, some being toppled, some being defaced. The statues that are being targeted are of people that protesters say shouldn't be memorialised. Some statues are of slave-traders, some are of Confederate Generals; even Christopher Columbus, who despite discovering America, (and the people already there), also sold women and girls into sex slavery.

(CH) China has reported the highest number of Covid-19 cases since April 13. There are 57 new cases today. 38 of the new cases were locally transmitted with 36 of them in Beijing. Health officials in Beijing have closed a street market after several domestically transmitted cases were confirmed as being related to the market.

(INDIA) India has reported its biggest single-day jump in cases. 11,458. This takes their total to more than 300,000. India is the fourth worst affected country in the world.

(NZ) New Zealand is getting closer to eliminating Covid-19 as the country has had no new cases for 22 days. Elimination will be achieved if the country reaches 28 days (two incubation periods) without any new cases.

(RUSSIA) There are 8706 new cases in Russia. Russia has the third highest number of total cases in the world, (behind the US and Brazil), with 520,129.

(UK) In the UK a statue of Winston Churchill has been boarded up for fears it will be vandalised.

JUNE 14 SUNDAY

(GLOBAL) The past three days have seen more than 400,000 new cases of Covid-19. The virus is spreading nearly twice as fast as it did two months ago. Over 430,000 people have now died of the disease.

(GLOBAL) Over 4 million people have recovered from the virus, (4,140,314).

(BANGLADESH) Since testing began in early April about 400 Rohingya refugees have been tested. 38 have tested positive and two people have died. The reported number might not be accurate because Rohingya refugees with symptoms aren't coming forward to be tested. Rumours are spreading within camps that if anyone gets Covid-19 they must be killed to prevent others becoming infected.

(CH) The Fengtai District in Beijing has put itself on a 'wartime' footing after a spike in new Covid-19 cases reported yesterday. The new cluster of coronavirus infections are centred on a wholesale market, sparking fears of a new wave of Covid-19.

(NZ) New Zealand has no more active cases. The last community-based transmission was 44 days ago. It's been 23 days since the last reported case.

(UK) The United Kingdom has recorded 36 deaths. This is the lowest daily amount since March 21.

JUNE 15 MONDAY

(GLOBAL) There are now more than 8 million cases of Covid-19 in the world. It's been a week since there were *only* 7 million cases. The virus is spreading faster than it did a few months ago, perhaps due to the relaxing of Lockdown restrictions and the continuation of protests around the world where Social Distancing protocols are not being adhered to.

April 2 (1 million cases)
April 15 (2 million cases)
April 27 (3 million cases)
May 8 (4 million cases)
May 21 (5 million cases)
June 1 (6 million cases)
June 8 (7 million cases)
June 16 (8 million cases)

(CH) Security checkpoints have gone up in Beijing after a spike in cases linked to the biggest wholesale food market in Asia. There's been nearly 2 months of no new infections. In the last 4 days Beijing has reported 79 cases. Schools and sports venues have been closed and temperature checks have been reinstated at malls, supermarkets, and offices.

(FRANCE) France has lifted travel restrictions for European Union Citizens, (except for Spain, and former EU country, the United Kingdom). EU Citizens will be able to enter France without 14 days quarantine.

(HIMALAYAS) 20 Indian soldiers have been killed in a clash with Chinese forces in a disputed Himalayan border area. It's the first deadly clash there in at least 45 years. Both sides have insisted that no bullet has been fired in four decades, and that 'no shots were fired' in this latest skirmish. There are reports that this clash was fought with rocks and clubs.

(NZ) New Zealand has no more active cases. The last community-based transmission was 45 days ago. It's been 24 days since the last reported case.

(NZ) In New Zealand the Marist College cluster has been closed. It was the second largest cluster in the country with 96 associated cases. Clusters are closed when 28 days have passed since their last active case completed an isolation period. There are 5 clusters still open in New Zealand. The Bluff Wedding, Matamata's Redoubt Bar, St Margaret's Residential Aged-Care Home in Auckland, the Rosewood Rest Home in Christchurch, and the Atawhai Assisi Rest Home and Hospital in Matangi.

(US) Due to Covid-19's interference with the movie making world, next year's Academy Awards have been put back 2 months to allow film makers more time to finish their movies. Movie theatres around the world have been closed and some films have had to push back their theatrical release dates, or lose them entirely, going directly to video-on-demand or streaming services. The catch is, to qualify for an Oscar, a film must have a 'qualified theatrical run' of at least 7 days. Netflix has opened a few theatres specifically to qualify some of their films. There is a possibility that the Academy Awards might change the rules and allow movies that are streamed to be nominated.

(US) The US Death toll has surpassed 115,000.

JUNE 16 TUESDAY

(NZ) After 24 days with no new cases, today New Zealand has two. Two women, recently returned from the UK, were given compassionate exemptions to leave the hotel they were being quarantined in, to drive over 700kms from Auckland to Wellington. They were not tested before leaving the Novatel Ellerslie Hotel. They are both from the same family and flew from the UK via Doha and Brisbane. They are currently self-isolating in Wellington.

(NZ) On top of the news of two infected women driving through the North Island, it's been revealed that two teenagers were given exemption from isolation late last week to attend a funeral in Hamilton. After the funeral they ran away. They have since been located.

(NZ) Because of breaches in security at our quarantine hotels, New Zealand has suspended indefinitely compassionate exemptions to attend funerals and tangis for people under quarantine restrictions.

(NZ) Despite the fact that there are 2 new cases today these are not community transmitted. They are related to people who have recently returned to New Zealand, so effectively the country could still be on the path of eliminating the virus in the community. It's been 46 days since the last community based transmission.

JUNE 17 WEDNESDAY

(NZ) It's been 47 days since the last community-based transmission.

(NZ) There are no new cases in New Zealand today.

(NZ) Prime Minister Jacinda Ardern says that the incident where two Covid-19 cases left isolation should never have happened and can not be repeated. 'It was an unacceptable failure of the system.' She has appointed the military to oversee all quarantine and managed isolation facilities.

(NZ) Regarding yesterday's two cases it's been revealed that a National Party member, Chris Bishop, assisted with the two ladies compassionate consideration to visit their sick mother. They were supposed to have been tested before leaving their hotel but were not. The two got lost leaving Auckland and were met by the two friends who had lent them the car they were driving. There was close contact with their friends for about five minutes before parting with a 'kiss and a cuddle.' About 320 people are being considered as close contacts. These are people on their flight and those that were in managed isolation with them. All of them are going to be tested and isolated until a negative result is received.

(NZ) The number of cases in New Zealand is 1506.

(NZ) The Matamata Redoubt Bar cluster has been closed. With 77 associated cases it was the third biggest cluster after the Bluff Wedding (98 cases) and Marist College (96 cases). New Zealand has four clusters still open.

(PERU) Peru has surpassed 240,000 cases, passing Italy's total number of cases, 237,828.

JUNE 18 THURSDAY

(GLOBAL) Here are the ten most affected countries in the world.

1 USA (2,231,444 Cases; 119,885 Deaths; 910,976 Recovered)

2 Brazil (955,377 Cases; 46,510 Deaths; 477,364 Recovered)

3 Russia (553,301 Cases; 7478 Deaths; 304,342 Recovered)

4 India (367,264 Cases; 12,262 Deaths; 194,438 Recovered)

5 UK (299,251 Cases; 42,153 Deaths; Recovered N/A*)

6 Spain (291,763 Cases; 27,136 Deaths; 150,376 Recovered)

7 Peru (240,908 Cases; 7257   Deaths; 128,622 Recovered)

8 Italy (237,828 Cases; 34,448 Deaths; 179,455 Recovered)

9 Iran (195,051 Cases; 9185 Deaths; 154,812 Recovered)

10 Germany (190,179 Cases; 8927 Deaths; 173,600 Recovered)

*The United Kingdom doesn't record their recoveries.

New Zealand sits as the 112th most affected country with 1506 cases, 22 deaths and, 1503 recovered.

(NZ) It's been 48 days since the last community-based transmission.

(NZ) New Zealand has one new case. A man in his 60s, who is in quarantine and has just arrived from Pakistan, has tested positive.

(NZ) The Rosewood Rest home in Christchurch, and the Atawhai Assisi Rest Home and Hospital in Matangi, clusters have closed. The Rosewood cluster was the deadliest in New Zealand with 12 deaths (out of the 22 people who died in NZ).

JUNE 19 FRIDAY

(GLOBAL) Today has recorded the highest number of Global daily cases of Covid-19 in a 24-hour period. 182,202 cases.

(CZECH REPUBLIC) Yesterday the Czech Republic reported its highest daily amount of cases in two months. 118 cases, the highest number since April 21. The Government has been relaxing rules since May, focussing on localised measures, rather than nationwide ones.

(ITALY) Scientists in Italy have found traces of Covid-19 in wastewater collected from Milan and Turin back in December 2019. This suggests that Covid-19 was already circulating in Northern Italy before China reported the first cases.

(NZ) There has been a shooting in Auckland. One Police Officer has been killed and another injured. A member of the public was also injured as the car carrying the shooter sped away.

(NZ) The Bluff Wedding cluster has closed. It was New Zealand's largest cluster with 98 associated cases. Two deaths were linked to the Bluff Wedding cluster. Only one cluster remains open in New Zealand and that's St Margaret's Residential Aged-Care facility in Auckland.

(NZ) It's been 28 days since the last reported case that didn't involve Border-managed facilities. That's two incubation cycles of Covid-19. Although there are still cases being reported these are from quarantined travellers that have returned to New Zealand. The country itself has eliminated the virus. All that needs to be done now is to keep quarantined people away from the rest of the population until they've done their 14-day isolation period and tested negative for the virus.

(NZ) It's been 49 days since the last community-based transmission.

(NZ) There are no new cases in New Zealand today but the country can expect more in coming days as quarantine testing is ramped up. There are still three active cases. New Zealand's total is 1507.

(NZ) A 24 year-old man has been arrested and charged with murder relating to the fatal shooting of a Police Officer in Auckland earlier today. He will appear in the Waitakere District Court tomorrow morning.

(UK) Prime Minister Boris Johnson says that he expects all children to return to class by September. Schools have been closed in the UK since March.

JUNE 20 SATURDAY

(NZ) It's been 50 days since the last community-based transmission.

(NZ) A woman alleged to be an accessory after the fact, to the killing of an Auckland Police Officer, has been taken into custody. Constable Mathew Hunt was shot dead yesterday. Another Officer was seriously injured. A man charged with Constable Hunt's murder has appeared in court.

(NZ) In New Zealand there are two asymptomatic cases today. Both are travellers who have arrived from India. They were both in managed isolation.

(US) In Tulsa, Oklahoma, President Trump gave his first rally since the Pandemic began. Everyone in the audience had to agree not to sue if they contracted Covid-19. Six of his advanced set-up team have tested positive for the virus. The rally was expected to have up to 20,000 people; 6200 attended.

(US) Florida and South Carolina have both broken their single-day records for three days running. Florida reported 4049 new cases while South Carolina reported 1155. More people in their 20s and 30s have been testing positive for the virus. Florida has all the makings of the next large epicentre.

JUNE 21 SUNDAY

(GLOBAL) The number of Global cases has passed 9 million. (9,042,968). Here are the dates we reached each million and the days in between:

> April 2 (1 million) 91 days (Since Jan 1st)
> April 15 (2 million) 13 days
> April 27 (3 million) 12 days
> May 9 (4 million) 12 days
> May 20 (5 million) 11 days
> May 29 (6 million) 9 days
> Jun 7 (7 million) 9 days
> Jun 14 (8 million) 7 days
> Jun 21 (9 million) 7 days

(AUS) In Victoria there were 19 new cases of the virus. 10 are believed to be a result of community transmission. From midnight tonight to July 12 Victorians will only be able to have five people at their homes. Gatherings outside will be restricted to 10. South Australia is reconsidering its decision to open its border with Victoria on July 20th. Queensland has said that anyone returning from Melbourne must self-isolate for 14 days.

(NZ) It's been 51 days since the last community-based transmission.

(NZ) Two new managed isolation facilities were activated in Rotorua as a result of Auckland reaching its capacity.

(NZ) There are two new cases in New Zealand. The number of active cases now sits at seven. New Zealand's total is now

1511. The death toll remains at 22.

(SPAIN) Spain has reopened its borders to visitors from most of Europe. British tourists will be allowed in without having to quarantine for 14 days.

(US) President Trump's campaign in Tulsa yesterday brought less than the expected crowd numbers. It was initially supposed that a lot of people avoided the campaign due to the risk of contracting Covid-19, but hundreds of teenage Tik-Tok users and K-Pop fans say that they're at least partially responsible for the low turnout. TikTok users and fans of Korean Pop music groups have claimed to have registered hundreds of thousands of tickets to attend the rally, as a prank; all with no intention of turning up. A spokesman for the Trump campaign said that Black Lives Matter protesters stopped supporters entering the rally but the low number of protesters outside seems to suggest otherwise.

(US) More than 51,000 residents and employees of nursing homes and long-term care facilities have died of Covid-19. This is more than 40% of the total deaths in the United States.

JUNE 22 MONDAY

(BRAZIL) Brazil has become the second country (after the US) to pass 50,000 deaths. The country has confirmed that they have more than 1 million cases of Covid-19.

(CH) China has suspended imports of poultry products from a plant owned by US based meat producer: Tyson. The plant has been hit by Covid-19.

(NZ) It's been 52 days since the last community-based transmission.

(NZ) The funeral for the slain Police Officer who was shot and killed on Friday will have to be delayed as family members fly in from overseas. As Auckland facilities are packed they will be transferred to Rotorua.

(NZ) Prime Minister Jacinda Ardern has announced that the Government is amending its health order concerning those in quarantine. It will require people to test negative for Covid-19 before being allowed to leave quarantine.

(NZ) The Government has extended the ban on Cruise-Ships to beyond June 30th. Exceptions will be made for cargo ships and fishing vessels. Any arriving ship crew will need to quarantine for 14 days if they have not been on the vessel for 28 days prior to docking.

(NZ) New Zealand has two new cases bringing the number of active cases to nine. The two cases relate to overseas travel. Both patients were in isolation hotels at the time they were diagnosed.

JUNE 23 TUESDAY

(GERMANY) The District of Gütersloh has been placed into regional Lockdown after 1550 people tested positive at a meatpacking plant. Authorities hope that the Regional Lockdown will prevent the virus from spreading.

(NZ) It's been 53 days since the last community-based transmission.

(NZ) There are two new cases today. The total number of cases is 1515.

(NZ) Aircrew, maritime crew and people who work at the border, (customs, biosecurity, immigration and aviation security) will be subject to regular testing. Also people presenting symptoms, even if they have no history of international travel or contact with returned travellers, may apply to be tested.

(NZ) Because of rising costs and complaints that taxpayers are copping the bill for people being quarantined in hotels, the Government is considering getting returnees to pay part of the costs of managed isolation.

(NZ) Epidemiologist Michael Baker has spoken out on our current case reporting process, saying that we should be focussing on our elimination status, instead of new cases in managed isolation. All our active cases are at the border, not in the community so we should instead be told that we've gone for 53 days without any local transmission, and we've maintained our elimination status.

(SAUDI ARABIA) Saudi Arabia has restricted the number of domestic pilgrims attending the hajj, to 1000 people, after barring Muslims from abroad. Anyone over 65 will not be permitted to attend the annual pilgrimage.

(SOUTH AFRICA) South Africa has announced that it will start clinical trials for a Covid-19 vaccine at Wits University. Wits University is collaborating with the University of Oxford and the Oxford Jenner Institute.

JUNE 24 WEDNESDAY

(INDIA) India has seen its highest single-day spike. 15,968 cases.

(NZ) It's been 54 days since the last community-based transmission.

(NZ) Health Minister David Clark and Director General Ashley Bloomfield have admitted that 51 of the 55 people who left managed isolation early on compassionate leave, had not been tested for Covid-19. Of the 55 granted leave, 39 have since tested negative, 7 won't be tested because of medical reasons or because they are children, 1 was a mistake and never actually left the facility, 4 are awaiting test results and 4 have not yet been tested.

(NZ) There is one new case in NZ today. Our total number of cases is 1516. Our death toll remains at 22.

(SERBIA) The World #1 Men's Singles Tennis Champion, Novak Djokovic, has tested positive for Covid-19. He set up a charity tournament (the Adria Tour 2020), with a bunch of famous tennis friends, and drew a lot of flak for not recognising Social Distancing amongst players or fans. Fans at last week's matches were packed beside each other. One of the players, Grigor Dimitrov, tested positive in the weekend, throwing the tournament into disarray. Djokavic, since catching Covid-19, has expressed that he is sorry. Over the past few months his anti-vaxxing views have become public and his wife has been heavily criticised for spreading the conspiracy theory that the rollout of 5G technology, has been responsible for the spread of the virus.

(US) Texas has recorded almost 6000 new cases today, the State's highest single-day increase. The nationwide Covid-19 resurgence has wiped out two months of progress, triggering warnings from health experts of an impending disaster. New infections across the United States have surged to 36,126 today, the highest level since late April, and the second highest total since the outbreak began.

(GLOBAL) Here's a list of the Ten Biggest Conspiracy theories related to Covid-19 currently doing the rounds:

1. It's all a hoax.
2. Covid-19 was caused by the roll out of new 5G technology.
3. Bill Gates created the virus so he could vaccinate whole populations and surreptitiously plant microchips under people's skin.
4. The virus isn't that bad. It's killing people that were going to die anyway.
5. The Government denies that Hydroxychloroquine is an effective treatment for Covid-19 because they don't have enough of it to give to everyone.
6. Those who deny that you can cure Covid-19 by ingesting or injecting bleach and disinfectants are only doing so because they are opposed to President Trump.
7. China created the virus in a lab close to the Wuhan market and it escaped.
8. The US created the virus and planted it in China.
9. All the precautions are overkill. Millions of people will have immune systems strong enough to cope with Covid-19 so there's really no problem.
10. It's a plot by the Democratic Party to make Donald Trump look bad.

People will accept a lot of things if it fits in with what they already believe or suspect. As some people don't believe what their Governments are telling them or that News Agencies are giving them the facts then they will ultimately turn to alternative sources of 'truth,' predominantly on the Internet. It's easy to create a Conspiracy Theory. All you need is a snippet of truth (or possible truth), which gives your theory some credibility, and then hang whatever rubbish you want from it. Some of it will stick, and some of it will spread.

JUNE 25 THURSDAY

(WHO) Dr Mike Ryan, head of the World Health Organisation's emergencies program, says that the pandemic for many of the countries in the Americas has not yet peaked. Many countries in the region have experienced 25-50% case increases in the last week.

(NETHERLANDS) Face to face professions, (including sex workers), will be allowed to open their doors next week. After the summer, football matches will be opened to the public but crowds will have to adhere to social distancing rules. There will be no singing or yelling. Singing and yelling is considered a sure way to spread Covid-19.

(NZ) It's been 55 days since the last community-based transmission.

(NZ) Health Minister David Clark is facing criticism for refusing to take any accountability for the border security fiasco, and has been happy to vocally shift the blame to Ashley Bloomfield, effectively, 'throwing him under the bus.' Bloomfield has become a popular figure in New Zealand and pivotal in how the country has combatted the disease, so it's understandably that there's a bit of an uproar when he's been blamed for Border mistakes, especially by someone who broke his own political party's Lockdown rules... twice. (During Lockdown David Clark went Mountain-biking and took his family to a beach 20kms away). Even the new opposition leader, Todd Muller, has called David Clark's treatment of Ashley Bloomfield a 'disgrace.'

(NZ) There are three new cases today, bringing the number of active cases to 11. Two of the new cases were in Christchurch, the other in Rotorua.

JUNE 26 FRIDAY

(AUS) Australia has recorded the biggest daily rise in cases in two months. Victoria had 33 people test positive marking 9 days of double-digit figures. Out of Australia's 279 current cases of Covid-19, Victoria has 200.

(NZ) It's been 56 days since the last community-based transmission.

(NZ) New Zealand has one new case today. This brings our total to 1520.

(NZ) Because of the current spate of bad weather in New Zealand it appears that the country could be coming into its flu season; which was delayed due to Lockdowns and social distancing protocols. The current definition for Covid-19 testing is: People are eligible if they have a runny nose, or a sore throat, or a cough or a fever. Due to the high volume of people presenting themselves to be tested as New Zealand heads into flu season, the Government may have to change this definition.

(US) The United States has had yet another single-day record with 37,077 cases reported yesterday. 2.4 million Americans have been infected and 124,000 people have died.

(US) Government experts in the US believe that more than 20 million Americans could have contracted Covid-19. This is ten times more than official counts. The estimate is based on serology testing used to determine the presence of antibodies showing whether someone has had the disease or not.

(US) 37% of Americans approve of the way President Trump has responded to the Covid-19 pandemic. That works out to about 120 million people.

JUNE 27 SATURDAY

(GLOBAL) The number of Global cases of Covid-19 has passed 10 million. 6 days ago it passed the 9 million mark. The number of people who have been killed by the virus is over half a million.

April 2 (1 million) 91 days (Since Jan 1st)
April 15 (2 million) 13 days
April 27 (3 million) 12 days
May 9 (4 million) 12 days
May 20 (5 million) 11 days
May 29 (6 million) 9 days
Jun 7 (7 million) 9 days
Jun 14 (8 million) 7 days
Jun 21 (9 million) 7 days
Jun 27 (10 million) 6 days

(WHO) According to the World Health Organisation, Astra Zeneca's experimental Covid-19 vaccine is probably the world's leading candidate, and is the most advanced vaccine in terms of development. The British drugmaker has already begun large-scale mid-stage human trials of the vaccine developed by researchers at the University of Oxford.

(AUS) Victoria has recorded 41 new cases. This is double the daily rate they had a week ago. While Victoria is finding it hard to control the pandemic the rest of Australia is easing restrictions.

(NZ) It's been 57 days since the last community-based transmission.

(NZ) 2159 people left managed isolation facilities between 9 June and 16 June. Of these, 1288 have tested negative for Covid-19, while 367 are still awaiting testing. 137 people were not eligible for testing for various reasons. 79 people have refused to be tested. The Health Ministry is still trying to locate 427 people who have left managed isolation.

(NZ) There are two new cases today, bringing the total number of active cases to 16. There are a total of 1522 cases.

JUNE 28 SUNDAY

(CZECH REPUBLIC) The Czech Republic has had its highest single-day increase since April 8, (260 cases). The country has had a total of 11,298 cases and 347 people have died.

(NZ) It's been 58 days since the last community-based transmission.

(NZ) There are four new International-travel related cases today. This brings the number of active cases to 20. New Zealand has had a total of 1526 cases.

(UK) Britain is going to stop the 14-day Quarantine period for people arriving from countries it now deems as low risk. They are using what is described as a traffic light categorisation for countries. Visitors from green and amber countries will not have to quarantine for 14 days. Red countries, if they're allowed in at all, will have to quarantine.

(US) Florida has reported 9585 new cases in a 24-hour period. It's a State record. Arizona recorded 3591 new cases, matching the existing State record set on June 23. The United States had 45,000 new cases last Friday. This was the largest single day number since the pandemic started. More than 2.5 million people in the States have tested positive for Covid-19.

JUNE 29 MONDAY

(GLOBAL) The Global death toll has passed 500,000.

(WHO) According to the World Health Organisation the number of cases around the world, (10.1 million), is about double the number of severe influenza illnesses recorded annually.

(KAZAKHSTAN) Kazakhstan is heading for a second Covid-19 Lockdown after failing to persuade the population to stick to safety guidelines after Lockdown restrictions were eased back in mid-May. Since mid-May case numbers have risen from 5000 to 38,000.

(NZ) It's been 59 days since the last community-based transmission.

(NZ) There are two new International-travel related cases today, bringing the number of active cases to 22. The total number of cases in NZ sits at 1528.

(UK) The city of Leicester will have certain Covid-19 restrictions re-imposed as its infection rate is three times higher than the next highest local area. Nonessential shops, pubs, and restaurants, will be closed from tomorrow.

(UK) The 2020 Wimbledon Tennis Tournament was supposed to start today but was cancelled back in April. It's the first time since WWII that the tournament has been cancelled.

JUNE 30 TUESDAY

(EUROPE) There is a report that the European Union has agreed to reopen external borders to 14 countries from tomorrow. The 14 countries are: Algeria, Australia, Canada, Georgia, Japan, Montenegro, Morocco, New Zealand, Rwanda, Serbia, South Korea, Thailand, Tunisia, and Uruguay. The United States and Russia will have to stay away.

(AUS) The Victorian Government has re-enforced local lockdowns across 10 different Melbourne postcodes as high case numbers continue to appear in the State.

(NZ) Foreign Affairs Minister Winston Peters has said that although New Zealanders will be able to travel to the EU it does not mean that EU residents can come to New Zealand. He also stated that if New Zealanders decided to take a holiday in Europe then it shouldn't be too much to expect them to pay for their 14 day Quarantine when they return home.

(UK) Britain wants to reach an agreement with New Zealand and Australia where we become classified as 'Green' countries, according to their Traffic Light grading system. This means that New Zealanders and Australians will be able to travel to the UK without having to go into Quarantine for 14 days.

(ANTARCTICA) Antarctica is the only Continent in the world with no cases of Covid-19.

(GLOBAL) No countries or territories reported their first cases in June.

(GLOBAL) There are still Countries and territories that have not had (or reported) any cases of Coronavirus. Most of the following are isolated island nations in the Pacific Ocean: American Samoa; Ascension; Christmas Island; Cocos Islands, Cook Islands; Federated States of Micronesia; Kiribati; Marshall Islands; Nauru; Niue; Norfolk Island; North Korea; Palau; Pitcairn Islands; Saint Helena; Sahrawi Arab Democratic Republic; Samoa; Solomon Islands; Svalbard; Tokelau; Tonga; Tristan da Cunha; Turkmenistan; Tuvalu; Vanuatu; and, Wallis and Futuna.

(GLOBAL) In the first six months of this year 223 countries and territories have had cases of the Coronavirus: Albania; Algeria; Andorra; Angola; Anguilla; Antigua and Barbuda; Argentina; Armenia; Aruba; Australia; Austria; Azerbaijan; Bahamas; Bahrain; Bangladesh; Barbados; Belarus; Belgium; Belize; Benin; Bermuda; Bhutan; Bolivia; Bosnia and Herzegovina; Botswana; British Virgin Islands; Brunei; Bulgaria; Burkina Faso; Burundi; Cabo Verde; Cambodia; Cameroon; Canada; Caribbean Netherlands; Cayman Islands; Central African Republic; Chad; Channel Islands; Chile; China; Colombia; Comoros; Congo; Costa Rica; Croatia; Cuba; Curaçao; Cyprus; Czech Republic; DR Congo; Denmark; Djibouti; Dominican Republic; Ecuador; Egypt; El Salvador; Equatorial Guinea; Eritrea; Estonia; Eswatini; Ethiopia; Falkland Islands; Faroe Islands; Fiji; Finland; France; French Guinea; French Polynesia; Gabon; Gambia; Georgia; Germany; Ghana; Gibraltar; Greece; Greenland; Grenada; Guadalupe; Guam; Guatemala; Guinea; Guinea-Bissau; Guyana; Haiti; Honduras; Hong Kong; Hungary; Iceland; India; Indonesia; Iran; Iraq; Ireland; Isle Of Man; Israel; Italy; Ivory Coast; Jamaica; Japan; Jordan; Kazakhstan; Kenya; Kuwait; Kyrgyzstan; Laos; Latvia; Lebanon; Lesotho; Liberia; Libya; Liechtenstein; Lithuania; Luxembourg; Macau; Madagascar; Malawi; Malaysia; Maldives; Mali; Malta; Martinique; Mauritania; Mauritius; Mayotte; Mexico; Moldova; Monaco; Mongolia; Montenegro; Montserrat; Morocco; Mozambique; Myanmar; Namibia; Nepal; the Netherlands; New Caledonia; New Zealand; Nicaragua; Niger; Nigeria; North Macedonia; Norway; Oman; Pakistan; Palestine; Panama; Papua New Guinea; Paraguay; Peru; Philippines; Poland; Portugal; Qatar; Réunion; Romania; Russia; Rwanda; San Marino; Sao Tome and Principe; Saudi Arabia; St Barth; Saint Kitts and Nevis; Saint Lucia; Saint Martin; Saint Pierre Miqueon;

St Vincent and the Grenadines; Senegal; Serbia; Seychelles; Sierra Leone; Singapore; Sint Maaten; Slovakia; Slovenia; Somalia; South Africa; South Korea; South Ossetia; South Sudan; Spain; Sri Lanka; Sweden; Sudan; Suriname; Switzerland; Syria; Taiwan; Tajikistan; Tanzania; Thailand; Timor-Leste; Togo; Trinidad and Tobago; Tunisia; Turkey; Turks and Caicos Islands; Uganda; Ukraine; United Arab Emirates; United Kingdom, United States Of America; Uruguay; Uzbekistan; Vatican City; Venezuela; Vietnam; Western Sahara; Yemen; Zambia; and Zimbabwe.

(GLOBAL) In the first six months of 2020 there have been 10,550,729 cases of Covid-19 in the world. 5,829,897 people have recovered, and 519,248 people have died.

(NZ) We have no new cases today!

(NZ) It's been 60 days since the last community-based transmission. Effectively covid-19 has been eliminated from New Zealand.

GLOBAL CASES

282: Jan 20.
500: Jan 23.
9000: Jan 30.
11,000: Feb 1.
28,000: Feb 7.
45,000: Feb 17.
100,000: Mar 5.
179,836: Mar 17.
300,000: Mar 22.
422,907: Mar 24.
558,500: Mar 27.
870,000: Apr 1.
1,000,000: Apr 2.
1,600,000: Apr 11.
1,777,666: Apr 12.
2,000,000: Apr 15.
3,000,000: Apr 27.
4,000,000: May 8.
5,000,000: May 21.
6,000,000: Jun 1.
7,000,000: Jun 8.
8,000,000: Jun 15.
9,042,968: Jun 21.
10,000,000: Jun 27.
10,550,729: Jun 30.

GLOBAL DEATHS

17: Jan 23.

170: Jan 30.

259: Feb 1.

565: Feb 7.

908: Feb 9.

1115: Feb 11.

2126: Feb 19.

3050: Mar 1.

5428: Mar 13.

7098: Mar 17.

19,193: Mar 24.

25,251: Mar 27.

43,000: Apr 1.

107,047: Apr 9.

108,867: Apr 12.

129,000: Apr 15.

203,331: Apr 26.

330,000: May 21.

430,000: Jun 14.

500,000: Jun 29.

519,248: Jun 30.

GLOBAL RECOVERIES

4803: Feb 11.
16,357: Feb 19.
45,122: Mar 1.
78,324: Mar 17.
108,930: Mar 24.
128,000: Mar 27.
194,191: Apr 1.
423,744: Apr 12.
889,049: Apr 26.
1,014,776: Apr 29.
2,109,704: May 21.
4,140,314: Jun 14.
5,829,897: Jun 30.

JUNE: A TEAM OF 5 MILLION

'We knocked the bastard off!'

So said Sir Edmund Hillary, arguably the most famous New Zealander of all time. He achieved his accomplishment with Tensing Norgay at his side, standing on top of the world. Below him, somewhere under the clouds, he had a small support team of fellow mountaineers, looking up. To 'knock our bastard off,' we needed a team of 5 million New Zealanders, and a lot of good fortune.

There were things running in our favour before the virus reached us. The most obvious being that New Zealand is pretty much in the middle of nowhere; already self-isolated and 2000kms from Australia, our nearest neighbour. We had no land borders to worry about, and not a lot of ways to sneak in. So once we closed the borders to International travel there was no easy way for the virus to enter.

Another thing running in our favour was the delay it took for the virus to inevitably arrive. This gave us time to analyse what was happening in other countries, and determine whether or not our approach to dealing with Covid-19 would run along similar lines. Just seeing how the virus was crippling Italy and the UK was enough of a heads up to let us know that we would have to use different methods, and beat this thing fast before it had a chance to set in. New Zealand doesn't have the largest population in the world. Thousands of people dying was seen as a possible reality. Hence the idea of 'going early and going hard.'

It's probably a gross generalisation but Kiwis tend to have a 'get in there and get the job done' attitude, by whatever means. We've been isolated from the rest of the world since day one so we've had to adapt and become independent, doing things our own way with what we've got on hand. The 'Number 8 Wire mentality,' we call it; where we look at a problem and use what we have to get the thing sorted, without relying on conventional means or standards, or what other people might be doing. In our Covid-19 response our Government called on experts in the field of Science and Medicine, and actually used their guidance in combatting the virus, pushing aside any showboating or attempts at political gain. They also put the health of the population above the concerns of the economy. Without people there is no economy. It will take time but the economy will come back. Dead people don't. Years from now various Governments will be remembered for the amount of people who died under their watch during the Covid-19 pandemic. Many people who had voted for the opposition, (the National Party), were impressed with how Jacinda Ardern and her Government handled the Covid-19 crisis in New Zealand. The polls showed such a rise in their popularity that it was enough to make the National Party worry about their chances in the upcoming September elections.

We're probably not as patriotically 'loud' as a lot of other nations but we are certainly a proud country, and proud of what we've achieved. We praise our sporting heroes and applaud the achievements of ordinary, (and extraordinary), Kiwis making their mark in the world. We feel a certain pride when we have a Lorde, or a Peter Jackson, Taika Waititi, Stephen Adams, or Scott Dixon, making it on the worldwide stage. That said, we don't celebrate show offs, and are quick to knock down anyone we feel is getting a little bit too carried away with their success and fame, or are rubbing it in just a little too hard. We're quick to bring them back to the real world. They could be world famous but back home they're just us, and we make sure that it stays that way. Weird eh? But that's what we do. And if you have a leader that feels like just one of us, someone who will pitch in and not be afraid to get their hands dirty, then they're easy to accept and listen to.

We were given simple instructions. So simple that every school child understood what needed to be done, and why. But it wasn't just that we were given instructions, lots of countries were, but our instructions were given in such a way that they never really felt like an order. They felt like a form of encouragement where every one of us was part of an important team, united in stamping out Covid-19. The daily briefings were aimed at everyone. Even the kids weren't forgotten. They were an essential part of the team of 5 million as well. Other countries may have scoffed when the Prime Minister deemed the Easter Bunny and the Tooth Fairy essential workers, but who cares what other countries think, as a population we were just grateful that the Prime Minister cared enough for the youngest members of our team to acknowledge them and include them in her briefings.

So, New Zealand had a plan. It was stricter than what we were seeing in other parts of the world, but understood as a necessity to get rid of a virus other countries were struggling with. And it was so simple: Stay Home, Save Lives!

Most of us did what needed to be done without question. Yes New Zealand might be a country of sheep, but we are also a country of shepherds, with a determination to protect the flock. In a sense there were 5 million sheep we each had to look after.

In any team you get the ones who can play the game perfectly, (lets call them Group One). These are the ones you want on your team because they give you a great chance of winning. You also get those who aren't quite so good at the game, people who might slip up now and then, (Group Two). It takes them a bit longer to figure it out but Group Two people ultimately become more of an asset than a liability, and they still give you a good chance of success.

And if you're unlucky your team will have those who want

to defy everything, (Group Three). In effect they want to throw the game. They don't want to be part of what the collective is trying to achieve. In any professional sporting arena these people would be cut from the team before their negative influence can spread.

Our team of 5 million had all of the above. Almost everyone was in the Group One category; a strong majority staying home and staying put. They were only going out for essential supplies when they needed to, and kept their distance when they did so. The lack of traffic on the road and the empty cities attested to the fact that the vast majority were following the instructions.

There were candidates for Group Two; those who 'quietly' broke their bubbles to visit extended family or friends. This 'bubble-mixing' was consensual. It had to be. Most of us wouldn't have tolerated anyone trying to breach our bubbles, so anyone entering had to be consensual. Everyone knew the rules, but the one concerning 'bubbles' was sometimes stretched a bit.

As for Group Three, we had them too. Thousands of them! The thing with the Group Three people was that their actions were so blatantly selfish and out in the open that they were easily seen. It was like they wanted to advertise their defiance. I think a lot of them didn't expect to be reported because New Zealanders tend to keep to themselves and not raise much of a fuss. But not this time! Millions of New Zealanders were not going to sit still and watch a small number of people ruin what the rest of us were trying to achieve. Especially considering that their actions were just likely to prolong Lockdown restrictions. Group Three members were more openly condemned than those who had contracted the disease, (which were mostly shown compassion in our attempt to be 'kind and nice'). It was understood quite clearly that the general public would not tolerate the actions of the Group Three people, and we let them know that quite vocally. Many were told pretty firmly by their friends and family to, 'pull their heads in and stop messing it up for the rest of us.'

Many of the Group Three people coalesced into the larger collective when they realised that New Zealanders weren't going to accept their bullshit. They'd tried it on, and to save face they decided to play the game with the rest of us, and try not to be remembered as idiots. Some couldn't do it. Some were fined, and some were arrested. But Group Three numbers diminished rapidly.

As did the number of new cases, to the point where, as of writing there are no active cases in the community. There are still cases at our managed border facilities, a sort of 'no-mans land' separated from the rest of New Zealand. But our community is free.

Covid-19 has been eliminated from the community! The last community-based transmission we had was on May 1st, over two months ago.

How long this lasts will be determined by how strong our border controls are. We have to expect that the virus will jump the fence eventually, as thousands of people are being repatriated home from overseas, many from countries where the virus is far from under control. Of those thousands returning it's highly probable that there will be Group Three's amongst them, not wanting to quarantine for 14 days.

Isolating for 14 days is a small price to pay when you consider the amount of time a Lockdown needs to bring the virus back under control. But those wanting to breach 14-day Lockdowns don't really consider other people. They just consider themselves and the imposition all these rules are having on their life. The selfishness of one person breaching their own, singular, self-isolation, could ultimately lead to Lockdowns for everyone. And we've been there already.

The team of 5 million worked hard to eliminate it, many losing their jobs in the process. We will welcome others returning from overseas to join our team if they just follow the rules. If they don't then don't expect to be welcomed home with open arms. The cost has already been too high.

New Zealand has become it's own small bubble. The outside world is still crawling with Covid-19. It wants to get in, and if it finds a hole, it will.

Jason Komene 4 July 2020

SIX MONTHS IN A LEAKY BOAT

No one would have believed at the beginning of 2020 that our world could be turned upside down in less than three months, and hundreds of thousands of people would be dead of an invisible enemy by June.

Before 2020 killer viruses belonged in the cinema, not in our world where advances in medicine and science should have been able to stamp them out long before they got out of hand. This wasn't the Middle Ages. Hell, it wasn't even like when the Spanish Flu hit the world after the First World War. This was the 21st century. We're better educated than our forefathers, with a much better understanding of germs, viruses, and bacteria than our predecessors ever had. Devastating diseases belonged in the past.

Obviously, with what has transpired, we weren't as educated or prepared as we thought. And what looked good on paper did not necessarily translate well to a real-life situation. Yes, we've advanced in Medicine and Science to the point where we can see and study something 0.00012 the size of a millimetre; but it hasn't stopped millions of people becoming infected. We know how the virus works; we know what it attacks, and where it attacks. We know how quickly it multiplies, its incubation period and the people most likely to die from it, but it still has us beat. Hundreds of laboratories around the world are working on a vaccine. The race to create one started even before the virus had an official name.

That an invisible enemy could bring down Humans, the most advanced species on the planet, seems too preposterous, even now, for many of us. We're at war with an enemy that we can't even see without the help of an electron microscope. It's like a nightmare out of a horror story. Covid-19 sneaks up on us, sometimes masquerading as a friend or family member, then invades our bodies and kills us from the inside. We're not used to enemies like this.

This nightmare invasion has hit almost every country in the world since the first reported cases in January. By February its effects had already swept across the entire globe, with countries scurrying to prepare for an epidemic. By March it had captured almost every country. Only those naturally isolated or quick in imposing strict border controls had not fallen victim to its onslaught. But none were unaffected. Every country was now under its grip, either directly or indirectly. April saw ongoing Lockdowns as the numbers of cases, already overwhelming, crept into the millions. By May hundreds of thousands of people had died. Despite this many countries began making their first tentative steps in relaxing the restrictions their countries had been enduring for months. Some misjudged it and saw spikes in the number of new cases leading to possible second waves of infections. Some were more cautious. June saw the world momentarily turn its back on the virus as attention was drawn to the murder of a black man called George Floyd, in late May. Black Lives Matter protests swept across the world faster than Covid-19, reaching places the virus never made it to. The protests continued through the whole of June, (particularly in the States). And all the while Covid-19 was there. Lurking. Looking for someone new to infect.

It's been a crazy six months.

We've seen businesses large and small collapse; whole industries destroyed by the virus.

The multi-trillion dollar tourism industry all over the world has collapsed, as restrictions on travel, between, and within countries has meant that no one can travel. No flights have meant Airlines have had to lay people off. And who knows when people will dare take Cruises again? Hotels and other Holiday accommodation options have gone under as customers are no longer seeking their services. Many Restaurants and Retail businesses have gone out of business as they close to protect their clientele. Live Sports and the industries associated with them have seen a substantial drop in revenue as people are forced to stay home. Likewise Music Concerts and Band tours are on hold for an indefinite period as most countries restrict groups to less than ten. Television and Film production has halted. Even if any films are somehow completed they can't be played in any movie theatres, as they are all closed. The Box Office Hit of 2020 doesn't exist yet, and might not at all, unless someone makes a movie of: 2020 The Year Of The Virus.

Six months down and the virus isn't slowing at all. In January Nations were put on alert when there were only a few dozen cases known. Now there are thousands of new cases a day and it's become the new norm. There's an acceptance that thousands all over the world will die today of Covid-19. The increasing numbers horrify us but maybe not as much as they did in the early months, when we were truly scared. The numbers may be higher now but their impact is probably no bigger than the initial shock we felt with the first thousand deaths, (or the first 100,000 cases, or the first million for that matter). Every fortnight there seems to be a new milestone, as if it's important to know that we've reached another million cases; or another 100,000 dead.

Over 500,000 people have died. Every one of them was someone's father, mother, son, daughter, brother or sister. They all had a name and a purpose but now they've been reduced to a statistic. We can't even really envision how big 500,000 is without some reference. In New Zealand 500,000 people equates to the population of the Wellington Region, (which includes our Capital City); in the UK, the city of Liverpool is just under 500,000. Sacramento in the US is about the same. All are well-known places, and the equivalent of their populations... gone to Covid-19. None of the 500,000 will receive the funeral they deserve.

The death toll will continue to rise. As will case numbers. No one needs a crystal ball to predict this. While we wait for the vaccine that is going to save us, time marches relentlessly on. It's a terrible thing but as I write this there are hundreds of thousands of people, currently virus-free, who will succumb to the disease and die before Christmas. All we can do is hope it's not us, or someone we know.

Although New Zealand has eliminated the virus it's still out there, chipping away at the bubble our country has formed around itself. Covid-19 is seeking a hole in our armour, a crack in the system, and as it's relentless its probably only a matter of time before it finds one. We're in a leaky boat. "We've just spent six months in a leaky boat," (to quote Split Enz). Calls to re-open our borders with infected countries are continuing to be thrown at the Government on a daily basis. New Zealanders from infected countries are returning home in droves, creating an already obvious risk. Really it has to be only a matter of time before the virus breaks through.

We've defeated Covid-19 once. When it breaks in will New Zealanders have the stamina to knock it back again, or are we over it? Will the team of 5 million do what we've already done once to eliminate the virus from our shores?

I hope so.

We know we can do it, but it comes at an enormous cost; and a lot of people have already paid heavily. Are we willing to keep paying the price? Or should we surrender?

We'll just have to wait and see.

Jason Komene 8 July 2020

ACKNOWLEDGE-MENTS

First and foremost, of course, thanks to my bubble companions: Liz and Logan. They knew I was working on something and left me alone long enough to complete it. (They still don't believe it's done). Scruffy and Sonic were a bit more demanding of my time but as they kept me company on so many late nights they can be forgiven.

Thanks also to my "essential' workmates, (Elaine, Carla, Uriah and Kevin), who must have thought I was a bit crazy going on about Covid-19 all the time. Unbeknownst to them our lunchtime conversations helped mould some of the content of this book.

Special Thanks must go to Reynard Gondipon. Without Reynard this book would probably not exist at all, and definitely not in this form. Reynard read the early drafts and wisely told me what rubbish to throw out, in his own gentle way. When things looked bleak Reynard was there to encourage me to keep going.

And, thanks to my friends and extended family. They didn't really help at all as none of them knew I was even doing this, but I didn't want to leave them out. They have always been very supportive of my endeavours so I thank them in advance. This will surprise some of them, while others will say: "About bloody time!" So thanks... wherever you are.

I would never have been able to complete this project without the Internet. I live in a small New Zealand town and practically work in a tin can. The Internet is sometimes my only link to the outside world. In a world where fake news and social media conspiracies are popping up everywhere it's important to know that there are still reliable news agencies we can turn to. Many news sites are suffering right now due to the financial impacts of Covid-19 and a bunch of them are asking for small donations in order to survive. We need their truth and I encourage you to support them if you can.

Thank you,
Stay healthy, Stay safe.
Kia Kaha,
Jason Komene July 16, 2020

SOURCES

JAN 1: 1NEWS; WHO. **JAN 2:** CNN; The Lancet; NY Times; 1NEWS. **JAN 3:** University of Sydney; Xinhuanet; BBC News. **JAN 4:** 1NEWS. **JAN 5:** ABC; BBC. **JAN 6:** BBC. **JAN 7:** CAN; ISNA. **JAN 8:** 9 News; Stuff. **JAN 9:** CNN; 1NEWS. **JAN 10:** 1NEWS. **JAN 11:** WHO; Xinhua News Agency; Express. **JAN 12:** Stuff; CIDRAP. **JAN 13:** CIDRAP; 1NEWS. **JAN 14:** 1NEWS. **JAN 15:** WHO; NZ Herald. **JAN 16:** Worldometers; Rueters; Stuff. **JAN 17:** ABC; **JAN 18:** BBC; Nikkei; BBC. **JAN 19:** RNZ. **JAN 20:** WHO; Worldometers. **JAN 21:** 1NEWS; Worldometers. **JAN 22:** 1NEWS; NY Times; Worldometers. **JAN 23:** NZ Herald; Worldometers. **JAN 24:** NZ Herald; France24; Stuff; NZ Herald. **JAN 25:** NY Times; Sydney Morning Herald; Rueters; New Straits Times; Worldometers; 1NEWS. **JAN 26:** Worldometers; 1NEWS; Washington Post; South China Post; NZ Herald. **JAN 27:** WHO; Montsame; NZ Herald; 1NEWS; Worldometers. **JAN 28:** Morningstar; RNZ; Stuff; BBC. **JAN 29:** Global Health Security Index; Wikipedia; Canadian Govt; 1NEWS; CNN; Worldometers. **JAN 30:** WHO; 1NEWS; CNN; Worldometers. **JAN 31:** 1NEWS; CNBC; South China Morning Post; NY Times; Worldometers. **FEB 1:** RNZ; Stuff; 1NEWS; NY Times. **FEB 2:** 1NEWS; Stuff; NZ Herald; NY Times. **FEB 3:** NPR; 1NEWS; Washington Times; Worldometers. **FEB 4:** NY Times; 1NEWS; CNN. **FEB 5:** 1NEWS; Washington Post. **FEB 6:** Worldometers; NZ Herald. **FEB 7:** Worldometers; Japan Times; NY Times; US Dept of State. **FEB 8:** Reuters; China Daily; Newshub; NY Times. **FEB 9:** NY Times; RNZ. **FEB 10:** WHO; NY Times; Stuff. **FEB 11:** Worldometers; WHO; CNN. **FEB 12:** NY Times. **FEB 13:** NY Times. **FEB 14:** NY Times; CNN; Worldometers. **FEB 15:** NY Times; BBC; NBC. **FEB 16:** TVNZ; NPR; Stuff. **FEB 17:** NT Times; 1NEWS. **FEB 18:** Wikipedia; Japan Times; Reuters. **FEB 19:** Worldometers; The Spinoff; South China Morning Post. **FEB 20:** Wall St Journal; CNN. **FEB 21:** Reuters; Wall St Journal; Worldometers. **FEB 22:** South China Morning Post; NY Times; Worldometers. **FEB 23:** Al Jazeera; France24; BBC; Wall St Journal. **FEB 24:** CNN; The Straits Times; Worldometers; Twitter. **FEB 25:** WHO; Wall St Journal; The Hill; Worldometers. **FEB 26;** WHO; USA Today; Worldometers. **FEB 27:** Reuters; Worldometers. **FEB 28:** 1NEWS; The Federal Council; Worldometers. **FEB 29:** Stuff; NZ Herald; CNN; Worldometers, **MAR 1:** Worldometers; 1NEWS; CNN; NY Times. **MAR 2:** Worldometers; NY Times. **MAR 3:** The New Daily; Worldometers. **MAR 4:** Stuff; CNN; Worldometers. **MAR 5:** Worldometers; Stuff; ARPHS; BBC; CNN. **MAR 6:** Worldometers; NZ Herald; CNN; SXSW. **MAR 7:** CNN; ABC; The Hill; Forbes; Daily Mail; Worldometers. **MAR 8:** ABC; CNN; NY Times; Worldometers. **MAR 9:** Washington Post; BBC; CNN; Worldometers.

MAR 10: The Spinoff; Worldometers; CNN. **MAR 11:** Wikipedia; CNN; Worldometers. **MAR 12:** WHO; NY Times; ABC; CNBC; Reuters; CNN; Mehr News Agency; NY Times; Worldometers. **MAR 13:** Worldometers; Financial Times; Formula 1; South China Morning Post; 1NEWS; US Govt; BBC; Worldometers. **MAR 14:** Rolling Stone; Stuff; RNZ; Newsroom; NY Times; Worldometers. **MAR 15:** Stuff; NZ Herald; 1NEWS; BBC; NY Times; CNN; Worldometers. **MAR 16:** ScienceMag; TheConversation; Xinhua; RNZ; Stuff; Worldometers; Vox. **MAR 17:** Worldometers; MD Anderson Center; Siouxsie Wiles; The Spinoff; Stuff; NPR. **MAR 18:** France24; CNN; NZ Herald; Stuff; Worldometers. **MAR 19:** NPR; Worldometers; Business Today; NZ Herald; Stuff; BBC. **MAR 20:** CNN; ABC; NZ Herald; Worldometers; 1NEWS; Stuff; NY Times. **MAR 21:** The Straits Times; Reuters; Stuff; Worldometers. **MAR 22:** Worldometers; NY Times; CTV News. **MAR 23:** NY Times; NRL; Stuff; NZ Herald; NZ Labour; Worldometers. **MAR 24:** Worldometers; NY Times; CNN; Stuff; NZ Herald; BBC. **MAR 25:** Stuff; NZ Herald; NZ Civil Defence; Worldometers. **MAR 26:** Insider; BBC; Stuff; Siouxsie Wiles; Worldometers; Vox. **MAR 27:** Worldometers; Wall Street Journal; Stuff. **MAR 28:** AP News; Stuff; Worldometers; BBC. **MAR 29:** BBC; Stuff; NZ Herald; Worldometers; CNN; BBC. **MAR 30:** NZ Herald; Stuff; Forbes; Worldometers. **MAR 31:** Seven Network; Monaco Tribune; NZ Ministry of Health; Stuff; NY Times; Worldometers. **APR 1:** Worldometers; NY Times; Stuff; ESPN. **APR 2:** Worldometers; 1NEWS; Stuff; Reuters. **APR 3:** MSN; Stuff; 1NEWS; NBC; Worldometers; Reuters. **APR 4:** NZ Herald; Stuff; Ahval; Worldometers. **APR 5:** Worldometers; NZ Herald; Stuff; MSN; National Geographic. **APR 6:** Stuff; Worldometers; BBC. **APR 7:** Stuff; NZ Herald; BBC. **APR 8:** National Geographic; CNN; Stuff; NZ Govt; NZ Herald; 1NEWS; The Straits Times; Washington Post; Amazon. **APR 9:** Worldometers; NRL; Stuff; NZ Herald. **APR 10:** Stuff; The Spinoff; Worldometers. **APR 11:** Worldometers; Stuff; BBC; NY Times. **APR 12:** Worldometers; Reuters; 1NEWS; NY Times. **APR 13:** YouTube; Stuff; BBC; The Wrap; NY Times. **APR 14:** ABC; Stuff; NZ Herald; NY Times. **APR 15:** Worldometers; Reuters; NZ Herald; Stuff; CNN; Washington Post. **APR 16:** Stuff; NZ Herald; Washington Post; US Govt. **APR 17:** Stuff; NZ Herald; BBC; Texas Tribune. **APR 18:** The Guardian; Stuff. **APR 19:** BBC; Haaretz; Stuff; ABC. **APR 20:** 1NEWS; Stuff; NY Times. **APR 21:** NY Times; BBC; 1NEWS; NZ Herald; Stuff; Reuters. **APR 22:** Stuff, Ministry of Health; ABC; National Geographic. **APR 23:** NZ Herald; Stuff; The Conversation; BBC. **APR 24:** Wikipedia; Reuters; Stuff; Worldometers. **APR 25:** Stuff; NY Times. **APR 26:** Worldometers; WHO; Politico; Stuff; Billboard. **APR 27:** Worldometers; Stuff. **APR 28:** Washington Post; Stuff; NZ Herald. **APR 29:** Worldometers; New England Journal of Medicine; The Lancet; NZ Govt; NZ Herald; Stuff. **APR 30:** NZ Herald; Stuff; Worldometers; Wikipedia. **MAY 1:** NRL; Stuff; BBC. **MAY 2:** Stuff; RNZ; Newsweek. **MAY 3:** 1NEWS; Stuff; NZ Herald. **MAY 4:** Stuff. **MAY 5:** Stuff; NZ Herald. **MAY 6:** Stuff; Worldometers. **MAY 7:** Stuff; BBC. **MAY 8:** Worldometers; Stuff. **MAY 9:** NZ Herald; CNN; NY Times. **MAY 10:** RNZ; Stuff; NPR. **MAY 11:** Stuff; RNZ. **MAY 12:** Reuters; Irish Times; Stuff; Worldometers; NY Times. **MAY 13:** CNN; Stuff; NZ Herald; Worldometers. **MAY 14:** Stuff; NZ Herald. **MAY 15:** Stuff.

MAY 16: 1 NEWS; BBC; NZ Herald; Stuff. **MAY 17:** Worldometers; Nikkei; Stuff. **MAY 18:** Stuff. NZ Herald; BBC. **MAY 19:** Telegraph; Japan Times; RNZ; Stuff; FDA; BBC. **MAY 20:** NZ Herald; Stuff. **MAY 21:** Worldometers; NZ Herald; Stuff. **MAY 22:** NZ Herald; Stuff. **MAY 23:** WHO; NRL; Worldometers; BBC; NZ Herald; Stuff. **MAY 24:** NZ Herald; Stuff. **MAY 25:** Stuff; NZ Herald; Time; NY Times; BBC. **MAY 26:** ABC, Stuff; 1 NEWS. **MAY 27:** NZ Herald; Stuff; 1 NEWS; Worldometers. **MAY 28:** WHO; NZ Herald; BBC; Stuff; NY Times; NBC; NY Times. **MAY 29:** Stuff; BBC; NPR. **MAY 30:** Stuff; NZ Herald; BBC; NBC. **MAY 31:** NPR; Stuff; ABC; Worldometers; Wikipedia. **JUN 1:** Worldometers; Stuff; AA; NZ Herald. **JUN 2:** Reuters; France24; Stuff. **JUN 3:** Stuff; NZ Herald; Reuters. **JUN 4:** BBC; Newshub; Reuters; Stuff; CNN; Worldometers. **JUN 5:** Stuff. **JUN 6:** WHO; ABC; NZ Herald. **JUN 7:** CNN; ABC; Stuff; Worldometers. **JUN 8:** Worldometers; Bloomberg; Al Jazeera; Stuff; BBC; NBC. **JUN 9:** NZ Herald; John Hopkins University; BBC; Stuff; The Spinoff; RNZ. **JUN 10:** MEM; Stuff; Newshub; The Newstatesman; CNN. **JUN 11:** Worldometers; 1 NEWS. **JUN 12:** BBC; CNN; Stephen King. **JUN 13:** Telegraph; The Statesman; Stuff; Worldometers. **JUN 14:** Worldometers; PMC; Telegraph; Stuff. **JUN 15:** Worldometers; Reuters; BBC; NY Times; Stuff. **JUN 16:** 1 NEWS; NZ Herald; Stuff. **JUN 17:** Stuff; NZ Herald; Worldometers. **JUN 18:** Worldometers; Stuff. **JUN 19:** Worldometers; Reuters; BBC; 1 NEWS; Stuff; Telegraph. **JUN 20:** NZ Herald; Stuff; CNN; NY Times. **JUN 21:** Worldometers; ABC; Stuff; BBC; CNN; NY Times. **JUN 22:** Worldometers; CNN; Stuff; RNZ. **JUN 23:** Reuters; Stuff; Newshub; WITS. **JUN 24:** India Times; NZ Herald; Stuff; CNN; NY Times; Facebook. **JUN 25:** WHO; DutchNews; Stuff. **JUN 26:** Reuters; Stuff; 1 NEWS; CNN; NPR. **JUN 27:** Worldometers; WHO; ABC; Stuff; NZ Herald. **JUN 28:** Reuters; Stuff; NZ Herald; NY Times. **JUN 29:** Worldometers; WHO; Reuters; Stuff; BBC; ESPN. **JUN 30:** NPR; ABC; Stuff; NZ Herald. Worldometers;

www.ingramcontent.com/pod-product-compliance
Lightning Source LLC
Chambersburg PA
CBHW051434250726 .
48655CB00001B/61